THE BRITTANY

Amateurs Training with Professionals

GLADE RUN PRESS

Printed at Versa Press, Inc.; East Peoria, Illinois

5 4 3 2 1

Glade Run Press
P. O. Box 160
Valencia, Pennsylvania 16059
(724) 898-9663
www.gladerunpress.com

Second Edition
Library of Congress Cataloging-In-Publication Data

The Brittany: Amateurs Training with Professionals
Martha H. Greenlee and David A.Webb.
p. cm.
ISBN 978-0-9743212-4-9
1. Brittany – Training.
I. Greenlee, Martha H., 1945–
II. Webb, David A., 1939–

To Brittanys

The little pointing dogs with big hearts,

boundless energy, superb noses,

and gentle dispositions

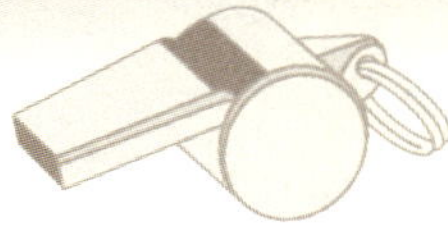

Contents

List of Illustrations

Preface

The Brittany: Amateurs Training with Professionals enables amateur pointing dog trainers to train hunting dogs that they are proud of and field trial dogs that win. While the emphasis is on the Brittany, this second edition of our book helps people who train any of the pointing breeds to become better trainers. The information in this book emphasizes a step-by-step training process and focuses on the logical progression of the steps.

This second edition has been more than fifteen years in the making. Soon after acquiring her first Brittany, Martha Greenlee began going to field trials, observing professional dog trainers and discussing their teaching methods with them. She listened and took notes, then went home and began using this information to train her dogs for hunting and field-trialing. Martha soon learned that some training methods worked better for her Brittanys than others.

At about the same time, Dave Webb was training his new Brittany pup. After reviewing all the extant publications on training pointing dogs, he found that most of them were written by or about professionals who trained breeds other than the Brittany.

Martha and Dave began comparing notes and discussing the lack of information available for amateur Brittany trainers. They took their concerns to several dog-training professionals and, with their encouragement and support, Martha and Dave embarked on the process of compiling a Brittany training book. The core of information in this book was derived from observations and discussions with seven professional trainers who actively handle Brittanys on the field trial circuit or specialize in training all the pointing breeds. The selection of these seven trainers in no way devalues the contributions made by other great dog trainers to this sport's body of knowledge. Martha and Dave chose these particular professionals because they are the ones with whom they have worked most closely, and their methods have been successfully used for training Brittanys for hunting and field-trialing.

This second edition is divided into ten chapters, and each chapter is divided into sections. Whenever possible, these sections describe specific professionals' training methods, and their names appear in the headings. However, when a section describes opinions or techniques held by more than one professional, no name appears in the heading. Authors' commentaries conclude the chapters and are the opinions of the authors.

This second edition retains most of the information from the first edition, as well as some important new material, including the addition of a seventh professional trainer, Maurice Lindley. Maurice's technique for using bird launchers to teach stop-to-flush is described in chapter 8, as well as how he starts the young dog to prepare him for formal training (see chapter 9). This edition also includes a section on gun safety (see chapter 4), and a discussion of scent and how to build a pre-release quail system is found in the appendixes.

Acknowledgments

The Brittany is a pointing dog that has unique attributes which set the breed apart from other breeds of pointing dogs. The Brittany has our heartfelt thanks for being a hunting dog, a field trial dog, a show dog, and a companion to all of us who love the breed.

We are grateful to the many people who have assisted us in writing this instructional manual. First, we thank the professional pointing dog trainers. Their creative technical training skills and willingness to share information were the impetus for our writing this book. Jim Basham, Bill Gibbons, Maurice Lindley, Ben Lorenson, Gene Stewart, Tommy Tracy, and Dave Walker reviewed a preliminary draft of the training sections and made invaluable contributions. The biographical sketches of the seven professional trainers appear at the end of this section.

Next, we thank Chris Cornell and Joe Arnett of Countrysport Press for their recommendations that gave focus and direction to this book. We also thank the following readers for their valuable and insightful comments: Ken Cherry, Tom Ettinger, Tom Greenlee, Russ Jackson, the late Dick Keenan, Cindy Miller, Chris Rider, Michael Siegel, and Joe Webb.

We appreciate Mark Anderson's artistic talents, which are reflected in the cover art and the line drawings for this second edition. Also, we wish to thank Esther Buchanan for her editorial expertise and review of the first-edition manuscript; Melissa Hayes for her editorial assistance with the second edition; and Lurelle Cheverie for her graphic design of the second edition. Last, but not least, we thank Alice Devine, Sherry Dinnen, Jean Ewers, Denise Giron, Nicole Ketter, and Emma Webb for their invaluable help in proofreading, both first and second editions, as the manuscripts progressed through various stages. In addition, Tom Frank and Chris Vandergriff assisted with publication aspects of both editions. Thank you, all.

We have enjoyed working on this project, and we hope that the information provided in this second edition of the book will be beneficial to you as you train your bird dog.

Meet the Professionals

JIM BASHAM

Born in 1936 in Cabin Creek, West Virginia, Jim was the oldest of four children. Faced with the prospect of following his father into the coal mines, he moved to Cleveland, Ohio, before he was eighteen and worked a number of odd jobs, including driving a Pepsi delivery truck and working as a short-order cook. He settled in as a millwright at the Republic Steel Company in 1957 and worked there until he retired in 1987.

Jim married Beverly in 1958, and they had two children, James Jr. and Sandra. Jim's involvement with dogs can be directly attributed to Sandra. As a toddler she was afraid of dogs. To help her overcome this fear, the family got a wire fox terrier and later, an Irish setter. In an effort to socialize the setter, Jim began showing him in conformation and obedience classes. When a friend commented that there was no way an Irish setter could compete in the field, Jim began training the dog and competing in field trials. Jim and the setter did so well that soon his formerly skeptical friends began asking him to help train their dogs. Jim began training dogs for other people as an amateur, but as demand for his services grew, his "hobby" of training bird dogs soon outgrew the family's urban setting. In 1972, they decided to move their operation to a fifty-acre farm near Nova, Ohio. That year, with two Irish setter pups, Jim attended his first field trial as a professional handler. By 1974 both setters were finished field champions.

Jim's first kennel was a converted chicken house with

ten runs that had to be closed in the winter due to lack of heat. These facilities, as inadequate as they were, did not prevent his hobby from becoming a full-time second job. In 1985 he built a forty-run heated kennel that allowed him to train dogs year-round.

Jim has finished over seventy field champions in nearly all the pointing breeds: Brittanys, English and Gordon setters, German shorthaired pointers, German wirehaired pointers, pointers, and Weimaraner. A number of these field champions went on to finish as dual champions. In addition to these accomplishments, Jim has handled and/or trained several winners of the Gordon Setter Club of America's National Field Championship.

Jim remains active in the training of American Kennel Club (AKC) field trial dogs. While nothing can beat the thrill of competing with a polished, finished gun dog, Jim says that bringing along young dogs and developing new talent still provides him with the greatest personal satisfaction.

BILL GIBBONS

Born in southern California, Bill was a year old when his parents moved to Arizona. He first started training pointing dogs—Vizslas—while he was in high school. After graduating from the University of Arizona in 1971 with a degree in agriculture, he spent the next several years in the military.

Bill and his wife Tamra now live in Phoenix where Tamra operates their grooming and boarding kennel, and Bill trains bird dogs. Their two sons (both grown and pursing their own careers) were accomplished trainers during their teenage years. Bill has been training pointing dogs as a full-time professional since 1973. He originally developed many of his techniques and methods under the tutelage of Bill West, and has trained and handled more than thirty Vizslas who won their AKC field championship or their American Field championship.

In 1996 Bill stopped traveling and competing in field trials. However, he continues to train all pointing dog breeds and says that there is no greater enjoyment in training bird dogs than working with pups. He has become a specialist in working out specific solutions to various problems that dogs have, including blinking, flagging, and being gun-shy. Many professional trainers do not have the time to correct such problems, but Bill does and loves doing it.

MAURICE LINDLEY

Born and raised in Greenville County, South Carolina, Maurice still lives in the same area. Even as a youngster, Maurice worked with dogs, although he wasn't introduced to bird dogs until the age of ten. That year, he and his brother went hunting with a neighbor who raised English setters. With the first point and covey rise, Maurice says he "was hooked for life" on pointing dogs.

Maurice and his brother soon saved enough money to buy one of the neighbor's setter pups. Since that day bird dogs and training have been a major focus for Maurice. He trained his first pointing dog, a German shorthair, for a client when he was sixteen years old. Today he and his brother, Bobby, are full partners in a boarding kennel, and they train all breeds of pointing dogs. Maurice is married to Kaye, who helps with the training and training seminars. They have one daughter, Sonya, and two granddaughters.

As a pointing dog trainer, Maurice has special skills with people and their bird dogs. He is a gifted teacher who is able to explain the reasoning behind his training techniques. He has trained pointing dogs for hunting, field trials, and hunt tests, and some of the dogs he has trained are handled by amateurs to compete in field events, including AKC, American Field, NBHA, and NSTRA.

BEN LORENSON

Born and raised in western Rhode Island, Ben began training dogs when he was thirteen years old. He trained a couple of bird dogs for a local professional trainer, and soon he had a full string of dogs. After he completed high school, he became a full-time professional trainer, mostly training gun dogs for hunters. Within a few years, Ben began competing in field trials, and he is one of the youngest professional trainers who travels the field trial circuit. The Brittany is the only breed of dog that he currently campaigns in field trials, although he trains all pointing dog breeds. During the summer months, he usually takes a few hunting dogs to train; however, his primary focus is the field trial Brittany.

For several years Ben and Tommy Tracy trained and worked together at Stone Ridge Kennels in Maine. On the field trial circuit, they were a tough team to beat, ably handling and scouting for each other's Brittanys when they were not braced together. Even after Tommy established his own kennel in Virginia, the two of them continued to work together when they attend the same trial.

Each year Ben's string of Brittanys consistently places and wins in AKC and American Field events. Ben says that he has lost track of the number of Brittanys that he has finished as AKC field champions. He has placed and won at the highest levels, including the National Brittany Gun Dog and the National Brittany All-Age Championships, as well as winning numerous all-breed American Field championships. Amateurs have handled dogs that he has trained, and placed or won at the highest levels, such as at the National Brittany Amateur Gun Dog and the National Brittany Amateur All-Age Championships, as well as numerous Amateur Championships.

GENE STEWART

When Gene was twelve years old, his dad obtained their first Brittany. Between the two of them, they trained, hunted, and field-trialed. More Brittanys soon entered the Stewart household, and in 1972 their first field champion earned his title. In 1980 Gene built a kennel and began training pointing dogs full-time. He has always trained by himself and is one of the most respected Brittany trainers in the country. Several professional trainers send their clients' Brittanys to

Gene to be steadied to wing and shot. He has worked and trained almost all the pointing breeds. Many of the pointing dogs he trains are for owners who want to have a finished dog for hunting.

Gene has trained over fifty dogs that he has either finished as open field champions, or the owners have finished as amateur and/or open field champions. He has judged many regional and several national Brittany field trial events, and continues to look for new and innovative techniques and methods for training pointing dogs.

TOMMY TRACY

Tommy owns and operates Cedar Valley Farms and Kennel in Virginia. He was raised in Connecticut and started working pointers with his dad, an active amateur trainer, when he was nine years old. Tommy said that his dad is the one who encouraged him to become a professional bird dog trainer. In addition to training dogs, he is an accomplished horse trainer, breaking and working horses for himself and other people who ride walking horses while handling and training their field trial dogs.

Being a shade on the other side of thirty, he is one of the youngest professional trainers who actively campaigns Brittanys on the field trial circuit. He became a professional at the age of seventeen, working with George Tracy in eastern Pennsylvania and then teaming up with Ben Lorenson. A few years ago he established his own place in Virginia. He has worked all the pointing breeds and has often trained pointing dogs for people who are only interested in hunting upland game birds.

For the past several years Tommy has done his summer training in South Dakota. He continues to actively campaign Brittanys during the fall and spring months, and each year his Brittanys have consistently placed and won in AKC and American Field events. Tommy has had numerous placements in all-age and gun dog stakes; has won the 1999 National Brittany Open All-Age Championship; was runner-up in the 2002 U.S. Open; won the Eastern Futurity in 2001 and 2002; won the 2004 National Gun Dog Championship; and won the 2004, 2005, and 2006 Deep South Brittany Free for All Championship.

DAVE WALKER

Born and raised in Pell City, Alabama, Dave owned and trained pointers and setters when he was a youngster. He did not subscribe to the harsh methods that were common practice at that time, and instead developed his own methods. Fundamental to his common sense approach to training dogs is the philosophy that dogs can't learn when they are in pain.

Dave spent twenty-one years in the U.S. Navy, the last eleven of which he was stationed in Boise, Idaho. While living in Idaho he trained bird dogs, and in 1964 he got his first Brittany. After retiring from the navy in 1973, he established a boarding kennel and began training bird dogs. In the early 1980s Dave sold his kennel business, and together with his wife Fay bought land near New Plymouth, Idaho, which they developed and named Walker's Plantation. Dave trains mostly Brittanys but also works with other pointing breeds, and Fay competes with Brittanys in the show ring. Between training and competing, Dave conducts seminars around the country, and has made instructional videotapes based on his methods (see appendix A).

Dave has trained and finished over 200 AKC and American Field champions and has won over 2,000 placements. He has won the National Brittany Open All-Age Championship three times, as well as many of the American Brittany Classics, including the Chukar, Pheasant, and Quail Classics. He has also won the Canadian All-Breed Shooting Dog Championship, and the Texas and Oklahoma Open Championships. In addition to these accomplishments, he trained and handled three dogs that have been inducted into the ABC Hall of Fame, and two that have been inducted into the Brittany Field Trial Hall of Fame.

Introduction

The history of the Brittany began thousands of years ago when people began to domesticate dogs and use them to help find, trail, and kill game for food. Eventually, four separate types of dogs evolved: the guard dog, the herd dog, the sight-hunting dog, and the scent-hunting dog. In addition to breeding these four types of dogs, people began to control the breeding of dogs for the purpose for which they were intended. Scent-hunting dogs were bred to be different sizes to hunt different types of cover, to have keen noses, and to have the ability to retrieve. Eventually, some of these dogs were bred to point upland game, while others were bred to flush.

Brittanys, the small, leggy pointing dogs, stand about 20 inches at the shoulder and weigh about 30 to 40 pounds. Other pointing dogs, such as English and Irish setters, stand about 23 inches at the shoulder and weigh 60 to 70 pounds. Brittanys are known for their exceptionally keen noses and ability to find birds. In France, their country of origin, they historically were known for being tough little individuals with excellent retrieving abilities. They usually belonged to thrifty French peasant farmers and were the hunters, guardians of the farm, and the family pet.

Pups were often whelped with short (bobbed) tails. There are many theories about the docking (cutting off) of the Brittany's tail. One popular theory is that the short tails proved to be advantageous because they were less likely to be injured when the dogs were hunting in heavy underbrush. As a result, owners began docking the tails of young pups. Ultimately, the docking of the tails became part of the breed standard.

Several reference books have been written about the origin of the breed, and a partial list appears in appendix D. *The New Complete Brittany* is probably the most concise summary of the Brittany's origins.

The Brittany spaniel is the result of the crossing of English setters with small French land spaniels. This process began as early as 1850, and possibly earlier. The English setter was itself developed from some of the swifter land spaniels of England, and possibly Wales. In the interior of Brittany, France, liver and white colors predominated. In the coastal areas, orange and white were prominent. By 1904, the Brittany spaniel had evolved into a distinct breed.

Within the rural Brittany province of France, the Breton peasants interbred setters, spaniels, and pointing breeds, and developed outstanding hunting dogs known as Braques. These excellent local hunting dogs were bred for their performance afield. Each year wealthy English sportsmen came to Breton to hunt with their well-trained dogs—predominantly English setters, Irish setters, and red-and-white Welsh springer spaniels. Often the English sportsmen left their hunting dogs with the local people to await the next shooting season. Undoubtedly, the interbreeding of the Braques and the English pointing and flushing dogs ultimately produced the Brittany spaniels. Juan Pugibet, a Mexican kennel owner of French ancestry, imported the first Brittanys (called Brittany spaniels in France) to the Americas in the early 1920s. His Casa Blanca Kennels bred excellent Brittany spaniels, which became the foundation stock in Canada, Mexico, and the United States. Most of the dogs were registered with the American Kennel Club, and many were also registered with the *Field Dog Stud Book* (FDSB) of the American Field.

The first Brittany spaniels came to the Americas to hunt. They were superb grouse and woodcock dogs. In the United States they quickly proved to be eager hunting companions. The breed proved to be equally successful for hunting quail, pheasants, and other upland game birds.

Because the hunting season lasts for a relatively short period of time, often owners of bird dogs who want to extend the time that they can work with their dogs participate in field trials. The first recorded entry of a Brittany in a field trial was in 1935. Over the years the popularity of these events has continued to increase.

In 1944, the American Kennel Club gave final recognition to the American Brittany Club. At the same time the newly formed club asked to have the name of the breed changed from "Brittany spaniel" to "Brittany." The American Kennel Club (not about to change the breed name from a source other than the country of origin—France) denied the request. In 1982 when the American Brittany Club once again proposed that the word "spaniel" be dropped, the American Kennel Club agreed to the change. Note that the Brittany spaniel name remains unchanged in many other countries, including Canada.

WHOEVER SAID, "YOU CAN'T BUY HAPPINESS" FORGOT LITTLE PUPPIES.

GENE HILL

CHAPTER ONE

Picking a Pup and Getting Started

If you have never owned a Brittany, there may be a number of different reasons for your choosing this breed. Possibly a friend recommended the breed to you, or you were impressed with a hunting partner's Brittany. Many people simply prefer Brittanys because they are the smallest pointing breed, they are great with kids and full of energy, and they have excellent temperaments.

For literary ease, the masculine pronouns "he," "his," and "him" are used in this book to refer to a single dog or trainer.

PICKING A PUP

Carefully choose your pup from a breeder who has a good reputation. Consider the bloodlines. Promise yourself to spend ten to fifteen minutes each day, almost every day, working with your pup. Remember, you are responsible for guiding your pup through his early months and years of training. Bring your pup home when he is at least seven weeks old. The possibilities of developing your dog for hunting or field-trialing, for the show ring, or simply for being a great companion are much better when you make the pup part of your family. A kennel-raised pup with little human contact does not develop into a well-mannered dog.

Your pup does not need to live in your home, but you do need to spend as much time as possible with him. You must become the central figure in his life; after all, you will replace his mother and littermates and become his best buddy. You feed him, you provide him with a place to sleep, you take him for walks, and you give him happy times. You are going to develop a relationship with your pup that will last a lifetime.

As the owner of a new pup, don't rush things. Serious hunting and field trial competition should be delayed until he is mature enough to deal with this type of training. Puppies need to be puppies and have fun. If you push him too hard with strict discipline too early, you can adversely affect his desire to hunt and compete in field trials.

How to Pick a Pup:
GENE STEWART

When Gene makes a recommendation for selecting a pup, the first questions he asks are: What does the buyer want from the pup? Is the dog intended to be used as a hunting dog, or is he intended to be a potential field trial dog? Gene also considers the traits of the dog's parents and grandparents when making a decision.

Hunting Dog With a hunting prospect it is important to observe the sire and dam. Notice how these Brittanys perform in the field. How do they range? How do they hunt? Would either of them be the partner you would want to take afield for an afternoon of hunting?

Field Trial Dog With the potential field trial prospect, however, Gene recommends looking closely at the grandparents as well as the parents. Have these dogs participated in field trials? Most importantly, do they have winning records?

SOCIALIZING

Behavior studies for dogs have shown that the first twelve weeks are extremely important, because a pup's experiences, during this time, will affect his emotional responses as an older adult dog. The need for human contact is important and starts soon after a pup is born. Research has shown that a three- to seven-weeks-old pup can be strongly affected by a lack of human contact, developing into a shy and easily excitable dog. It is important for breeders to spend a lot of time with their pups during the early formative stages of their lives.

When you take your pup home, the responsibility now becomes yours. While you should certainly fuss over him and make him your buddy, this is also the time for you to begin teaching him that you are the boss. When you cradle him in your arms, hold him quietly until he relaxes. You should practice this lesson two or three times a day, making each session last about two or three minutes. If he struggles, do not put him down. Wait until he stops struggling. In this simple way you are beginning to establish your authority.

Take him with you everywhere you go. Put a collar and leash on him and take him for walks. Put him in a kennel crate and take him for rides in your car. Let him be around other people, especially kids. Let him sort out the multitude of smells, sounds, and sights and determine their importance. *Caution:* Do not expose him to loud noises, such as Fourth of July fireworks. (See chapter 3, Introducing Birds and Gunfire.)

If there is an obedience club in your area, find out if it offers kindergarten classes for puppies. If they are available, take your pup to these classes. They are fun for the whole family and provide you with important information and support. You learn to recognize average puppy behavior of all breeds. The commitment to the class ensures that you are spending time training your pup, and your pup receives both canine and human socialization.

The importance of socialization cannot be overemphasized. Socialization begins with the breeder and must continue with you as the pup's new owner. Take your pup to all sorts of new and different places: to the post office, to the bank, for walks in the park on a lead, and so on. Puppies attract people's attention, so take advantage of every opportunity to stop and let people pet and play with your pup. These experiences develop his self-confidence and his trust in people.

CRATE TRAINING

Crate training is a simple process of introducing your pup to a crate and is one of the most important steps in teaching him to become a well-mannered dog. Besides a leash and collar, a crate is one of the most important pieces of equipment you need when you bring your pup home. This is where he sleeps at night, where he stays during the day for short periods of time when he can't be supervised, and where he rides in your car when he travels with you.

If you haven't used a crate before, you may think that confining a pup in a crate is cruel. It isn't. Remember that the Brittanys' ancestors were den-dwelling animals. Watch your pup when he lies down to take a nap. Instinctively, he finds a protected spot. A crate simulates a den and offers security, privacy, and protection.

For the first couple of weeks your job is to get your pup accustomed to the crate. Like every aspect of dog training, introduce it to him in stages. Let him investigate the crate by leaving the door open so that he can go in or out. Put a treat or toy in there and let him find it. Keep the crate in a busy area during the day—one where you or other people are working—and leave him in it for short periods. At night move the crate into the bedroom so that he can sleep near you. If he cries when you crate him, ignore him. He will stop eventually. If you feel sorry for him and let him out, you are rewarding him for crying, and he will only cry more. Always wait until he is quiet before letting him out.

Crate training is also useful for housebreaking. A pup instinctively doesn't want to soil in his den, so he learns to "hold it." Young puppies may not be able to hold it through the night and may need to be let out, but you will be surprised at how easy housebreaking is when you use a crate.

If your pup starts to get into everything or seems uncontrollable, use the crate to help you maintain control. However, you should never use the crate for punishment. Remember—the crate is where he feels safe. As he gets more comfortable with the crate, begin to say *Kennel* and give him a treat when he goes into his crate. Eventually, you will give the kennel command and he will go into his crate. Leave the door open, and he may surprise you by going into the crate when he wants to take a nap.

There are many different styles and sizes of crates. Crate styles include the plastic airline type and others that are all wire. The plastic airline crate offers more security and is the most popular type. If you choose a wire crate, put a blanket over the crate to keep out the light. The size of the crate depends on the size of your dog. It should be large enough to allow him to lie down, to stand up (with sufficient shoulder clearance), and to turn around. If the crate is too large, it loses its housebreaking effectiveness because your pup can defecate in it. Full-grown Brittanys generally require an intermediate-size crate, one about 22 inches wide by 32 inches deep by 23 inches high. Many people buy a crate to fit their adult dog and then block off the back half with a piece of plywood while their pup is small.

EARLY TABLE TRAINING

The next step in early training of your pup is working with him on a table—whether it be a training table, a picnic table, the tailgate of your truck, or a bench. If the surface is slick, put down a piece of carpet to give him a firm footing. Begin to teach him to stand still and to let you touch him. As you continue to work with him on a table, you notice that he begins to settle down more quickly than he did when you first began training.

First, stand him on the table. If he becomes nervous or acts worried, give him a treat to let him know that good things happen to him when he is on the table. In the beginning it is best to work him in short sessions, ranging from one to two minutes. Once he seems relaxed, begin to restrain him, but do not use undue force. Keep him standing in one position. Stroke him over his entire body. As you pet him, gently open his mouth. Touch his ears and eyes. If you do something that makes him act nervous or worried, back off and do something that he's comfortable with. Pick up his feet and hold them, one at a time. If he struggles, do not let go. Hold his foot until he calms down; otherwise, you are rewarding him for struggling. Eventually, he learns to trust you, and the bond between the two of you is strengthened.

■ ■ ■

AUTHORS' COMMENTARY

Four elements are key to raising a pup that becomes a well-mannered dog:

1) Get your pup from a reputable breeder.
2) Provide him with appropriate socialization.
3) Crate-train him.
4) Touch and handle him.

Raising a puppy can be a joyous experience, but it's important to remember that most dogs do learn some bad behaviors as puppies. Preventing your pup from developing a bad behavior is far easier than stopping this behavior *after* he develops it. For example, if your pup is creating havoc in the house, crating him helps stop it. Be vigilant as well as diligent. Stop bad behavior as soon as it starts.

Maintain your pup's health by taking him to a good veterinarian. Keep him up to date on vaccinations and preventive medications, such as heartworm pills. Talk to your vet about any problems your pup is having, either physical or behavioral; he may be able to suggest some positive solutions.

Allow your pup freedom to enjoy a variety of experiences, but don't overreact when he misbehaves, and don't expect perfection. A puppy is forever forgiving. If you make his life enjoyable, he will think you are wonderful, and he will want to please you.

■ ■ ■

TO MAKE A GUN DOG, YOU NEED BIRDS – BIRDS AND MORE BIRDS.

GENE STEWART

CHAPTER TWO

Using Birds for Field Training

You need birds for most of the field training that you do with your Brittany. This training includes:

- introducing him to birds;
- introducing him to gunfire;
- teaching him a pattern;
- teaching him to be steady-to-wing-and-shot; and
- providing additional training, such as stop-to-flush, backing, and retrieving.

Historically, bird dogs were trained on wild birds, but there are only limited areas within the United States that still have significant populations of wild birds. Furthermore, there are times when you want to control the location of the birds. Most professionals buy pen-raised birds, although some pigeons may be trapped. There are many types of pen-raised birds, including pheasant, chukar, and Hungarian partridge. Some of these birds may be excellent for training a young dog; however, they are expensive. The two most commonly used birds are pigeons and quail.

If you are fortunate enough to have access to wild birds, hunt your pup on them as often as possible. If you are like most amateurs, you will train mostly on pen-raised birds, and the way in which you present these birds to your dog is important. Many training problems occur as a result of birds not acting naturally, as wild birds would respond. Even though pen-raised birds are not wild, their actions should be as close as possible to that of wild birds. When you are ready to buy birds, be prepared to shop around. Look for a game bird breeder who sells healthy birds that are flight-conditioned. Plant them where wild birds would normally be found. You want birds that get up and fly when they are flushed, and have as little human scent as possible on or around them. Some professionals recommend wearing gloves when handling birds; others do not. All agree that the less the birds are handled, the better.

TRAINING WITH PIGEONS

Pigeons are ideal training birds for the single dog owner. They are easy to find and may be kept in a small wire pen for a week or in a pigeon coop for a longer period of time. Get a how-to book to learn how to take care of pigeons and how to build a pigeon coop (see appendix A).

Pigeons do not hold for a pointing dog and must be restrained to prevent them from flying away. Some trainers recommend putting a pigeon to sleep by tucking its head under its wing before planting it. This sleepy condition keeps it from flying for a short period of time, but a sleepy bird doesn't act naturally, and this unnatural action causes training problems. A dog learns he can crowd the pigeon (move too closely to it) because it doesn't get up. He also learns that he can follow the bird planter's tracks to the bird and find it without having to hunt. One of the best ways to plant a pigeon is to tether it by tying a piece of cardboard or a short length of garden hose to one of its legs. A tethered pigeon acts naturally. A dog learns he can't crowd the bird because it flushes if he gets too close. The bird is able to fly a short distance before landing, and there are no tracks leading to the bird for the dog to follow.

Tethering a Pigeon

HOW TO TETHER A PIGEON: David Walker

To make a tether, Dave cuts an 8x10-inch section from the side of a cardboard box. In one corner he punches a hole. Next, he cuts a piece of yarn about 18 inches long, doubles it, and ties the two ends together. He pushes one end of the doubled yarn through the hole, separates it to make a loop, and takes the other end and puts it through the loop to form a half hitch between the hole and the edge of the cardboard. Then Dave forms another half hitch with the tag end of the yarn and slides it over one of the pigeon's feet. Tying the tether to one foot puts the pigeon off balance. The bird is able to fly a short distance before it is forced to land. In windy conditions birds fly farther. If the birds are flying too far, Dave pulls a couple of flight feathers from only one wing, causing the bird to fly in a circle.

Dizzying a Pigeon

To dizzy a bird, hold the bird by the body and spin the head in small, fast circles until the head droops to the side.

Another way to plant a pigeon is to put it in a bird launcher (see appendix A). A launcher is a metal box with springs that releases the bird manually or remotely. The manual launcher has a release lever on the side that has to be depressed to open the launcher. A string can be tied to the lever and laid on the ground near where you plan to stand to launch the bird. The remote launcher has electronics added to it, so you can release the bird with a transmitter from any direction. Distance varies with manufacturers. Launchers are great tools for teaching a dog to "stop and stand still" at the flush of a bird he can't see or smell, but be aware that problems may arise if your dog is allowed to point them too often. Because birds are not moving around, your dog doesn't develop the skills to find loose birds. Also, he may learn to follow your tracks to the launchers.

Using Tethered Pigeons:
DAVE WALKER

Dave uses cardboard tethers to plant pigeons, so he can use the same birds repeatedly in a training session. Cardboard is light and doesn't tire the bird as much as garden hose. Dave takes two or three birds and attaches the cardboard. Then he walks to the area where he wants to have bird work. To prevent the bird from flying too far from where he releases it, Dave dizzies the bird until its head droops, and then he gently tosses the bird sidearm, like a baseball. The bird will fly a short distance and land. By using this procedure, there are no foot tracks to the bird, and the bird is awake and alert and can fly if crowded by a dog.

Dave trains in a large open field. The area is mowed so that there are alternating strips of cover and cleared areas. The cover in the strips conceals the birds from a dog's view. Dave tries to keep the pigeons away from trees because the cardboard can get hung up in them.

Using Bird Launchers: MAURICE LINDLEY

Maurice uses bird launchers to secure pigeons and plants them in light cover where the dog can't see them. The birds are awake and alert and fly back to the coop when the launchers open.

Before a launcher is ready to use, Maurice adjusts the springs. If the launcher comes with adjustable springs, Maurice adjusts them to the lightest tension. If the launcher does not adjust, Maurice replaces the springs with light tension springs. He wants the launcher to open and the bird to get up, so it looks natural and not thrown. Also, light springs are quiet, so the launcher doesn't spook the dog when it opens.

New birds need to be conditioned to launchers by launching them a couple of times for practice before using them in training. The birds are ready when they fly as soon as the launchers open.

TRAINING WITH QUAIL

Brittanys love the smell of quail. Depending on your region of the country, if your pup is a hunting pup, he may never have the opportunity to hunt wild quail, but exposure to pen-raised quail helps him learn to use his nose and the wind. If your pup is a field trial pup, he will probably be worked on quail most of his life. Often quail are the first birds a young pup smells, and they are used in many phases of training throughout his career.

Quail are available year-round from game bird breeders. They can be housed in a small wire pen for a week or in a quail house for longer periods. Catalogs are available listing books and videos that explain how to care for quail and how to build a quail house (see appendix A).

Planting Quail

To plant quail individually, use the same procedure that Dave Walker uses for dizzying a pigeon. Dizzy the quail until its head droops and toss it into some type of protected cover such as a hedgerow, tree line, or bushy objective. You want to plant your birds in places where wild birds might naturally be found.

To plant quail in small coveys of two or three birds, put the birds in a box, wire pen, or bird bag and take them to an area that you want to do bird work. Place the container on the ground, open it, and take a couple of steps back. Let the birds walk out into cover. Pick up the container and quietly walk away. You can spread feed around the area prior to releasing the birds to encourage them to remain nearby. Use the same feed that the birds are accustomed to eating so that they will recognize it as food. Before beginning bird work, wait thirty minutes to allow scent from your foot tracks to dissipate. You do not want to leave trails for your dog to follow to the birds.

Planting birds in coveys is better than planting them individually. If the weather is hot, or if scenting conditions are poor, a dog can smell two or three birds more easily than he can smell one quail. Furthermore, two or three birds are more likely to stick around because they aren't looking for their mates. Plant the coveys in habitat where quail naturally are found so the dog learns to recognize and hunt the productive types of cover.

If you have fifty or more acres to train on, you might consider a pre-release quail program. Pre-released birds are birds that are released into the environment a few weeks prior to being worked rather than planted birds that are put out and worked the same day. Pre-released birds are usually placed in some kind of protective structure, which is open enough to allow them to come and go freely and where water and feed are available. These birds are left undisturbed for a couple of weeks to form coveys and develop survival skills that include learning to eat native seeds and bugs and finding covers to protect them from predators. As they become proficient at these skills, they begin to mimic the behaviors of wild birds. Instructions for how to build a pre-release system for quail can be found in appendix B.

AUTHORS' COMMENTARY

As you know, many training problems are the result of working with pen-raised birds. The dog learns that he can crowd the bird or that he can follow your tracks to find the bird. These bad habits never develop in dogs that are worked on wild birds. If you use pen-raised birds, make sure that they are strong fliers, and continually compare the performance of your birds to that of wild birds. They may never explode into flight like wild birds, but keep the image in your mind because you want them to act as naturally as possible.

Not every day is a good day to train, even with the best pigeons or quail. If the conditions are wet or rainy, wait and train another day. Wet ground holds the scent, and wet birds don't fly well. If you work your dog in these conditions, he may learn to follow your trails to the birds, and he may learn that he can catch the birds.

THE NOSE IS LIKE A MUSCLE.
IT HAS TO BE WORKED TO DEVELOP.

BEN LORENSON

CHAPTER THREE

Introducing Birds and Gunfire

As the owner of a Brittany pup, you are responsible for preparing him to hunt. Two of the most important steps in his training are introducing him to birds and introducing him to gunfire. These two steps are the foundation of his future training and are key to training a dog you will be proud of. This is the time that his desire to hunt takes form and where he learns to enjoy his work. Remember that a puppy has a short attention span, so train him in fifteen-minute sessions, being careful not to tire him out or to let him lose interest. Also included in this chapter is a short piece on why dogs point, as well as a brief discussion of scent.

INTRODUCING BIRDS

The age that you introduce your pup to birds depends on his personality. If he is bold, you might introduce birds to him at three or four months old, but if he is timid you should wait until he is five or six months old. Your pup should be confident running on different types of terrain before you introduce him to birds. He may be self-assured in the yard, but he also needs to be self-assured afield. If he acts unsure in any way when he is out running, he is not ready to be introduced to birds.

Once your pup is running with confidence on different terrain and in different covers, you can begin to introduce him to quail or pigeons. Match the size of the bird to the size of the pup. Small birds (quail) work best for small (young) pups. Larger birds (pigeons) work well for larger (older) pups. The flapping wings of a pigeon may hit a small pup in the face and frighten him. Be observant. If he acts uncertain or if he hesitates or looks back at you at any time during the introduction, his reactions are telling you that he is not yet ready for bird work. Let him get a little older before you try to introduce him to birds again.

Introducing Birds to a Young Pup

If your pup is three to five months old, you should begin with quail. Here are the steps to follow with early training:

- Take two or three good flying quail to a small field.
- Dizzy each bird and toss it down along a tree line where there is enough cover to hold it.
- Plant each bird separately so that you have two or three objectives (likely covers for holding birds that a dog runs to and hunts).

Get your pup, but don't take him directly to a bird. Let him run free and hunt on his own. He is still young enough to want to go with you. Walk in the general direction of a bird, but don't call him or in any way indicate where the birds are. You have two or three chances for bird work, and you want to work him on only one bird. If he misses the first bird, you don't have to call him back over ground he has already hunted. Continue to walk to the next bird.

Once he finds a bird, he may point it, pounce on it, bark at it, and so forth. Whatever he does, let him do it on his own. If the bird flies, let him chase it. If he starts to chase but stops and looks back at you or comes back to you, he is telling you he is unsure. Wait a week before working him on birds again.

Be quiet while your puppy learns about birds and scent. These lessons are between the pup and the birds. By being quiet you neither indicate your approval nor your disapproval. Continue to work him on birds as long as he is not catching them, and you can pick him up at the end.

Puppy Stalking a Quail:

Be quiet while your puppy learns about scent.

PICKING UP A PUP AFTER BIRD WORK

Some pups may become hard to pick up after they've been chasing birds. The best way to pick up a three- to five-month-old pup after working him on birds is to sit down on the ground and wait for him to find you. You might have a treat in your pocket. Eventually, he gets tired of chasing birds, worries about where you are, and comes looking for you. You want to be close enough for him to find you but far enough away from him so that he has to look for you.

Some pups become more independent when they are about five months old and are beginning to mature. At this stage in his development, he goes with you, but he doesn't come to you. To help catch an independent pup, tie a light 6-foot cord (clothesline) to the pup's collar. If he makes a swing near you but isn't close enough for you to grab, step on the cord. Be sure to introduce him to the cord in advance by letting him drag it for a week before you use it to stop him.

It is important not to call him to you if you know he is not going to come. As with any command, do not use it if you can't enforce it. This is the quickest way to teach a pup not to listen. Call him to you only when you know he will come or when you're confident that you can catch him.

Introducing Birds to an Older Pup

If your pup is five months or older, you can work him on pigeons. A pup this age needs to catch a bird and get it in his mouth to taste it. Pigeons don't hold as well as quail and fly away unless tethered in some way. Here are some important steps to follow:

- Make a cardboard tether and tie it to one of the pigeon's feet.
- Dizzy the pigeon and toss it down in a small piece of cover in an open field.
- Keep the pigeon away from trees because the tether can get hung up in them.

Get your pup and attach a check-cord to his collar. The check-cord referred to in this book is a stiff rope, about 1/2 inch in diameter and approximately 12 feet long, with a swivel snap at one end (discussed in detail in chapter 5, Beginning Yard Work). At this age you need to have physical control of him, but he may not listen to you. If he has never had a check-cord on, walk him around until he gets used to it. Once your pup is comfortable hunting at the end of the check-cord, bring him in to the bird downwind and across the scent. If he points the pigeon, quickly walk in and flush it. If he dives for the bird, stop him with a gentle tug on the check-cord to prevent him from catching it. You want him to catch the bird *after* it has flown. Once it flies, drop the check-cord and let him chase it, or hold the check-cord and run with him in the direction the bird is flying. When the bird lands, let him catch it or do whatever he wants to do with it. Once your pup starts to lose interest in the pigeon, take the check-cord, turn, and walk in a different direction. Encourage him to go with you by pulling the check-cord with quick, gentle tugs. Praise him if he brings the bird to you, but don't make a big deal out of it if he doesn't.

Why Dogs Point:
BILL GIBBONS

After reading Bill Gibbons's explanation of why dogs point, observe your own dog. Do you recognize the stages Bill describes?

> Why does a dog point a bird and why is he intense on a bird, or a rabbit, or a fly? Why is he intense, and why does he lose that intensity? Because he can't catch them. He first smells a bird and the bird takes off running or flies and that dog thinks, "Boy, I'm going to get him." Well, then he doesn't get him. So he finds him another one, and runs him again. Boy, he's having a great time. Finally he starts getting kind of tired. In a normal situation, it isn't long before he'll smell a bird and freeze. Why is he not just ripping out and chasing it?
>
> ***Stalking***. Dogs that point are stalking. Everybody's seen a cat moving out in the field and then freeze. For a long time he freezes. Then he's trying to get close again to pounce on his prey, to catch it. The only thing that's natural to a dog, really, is his desire to hunt, to find something hunted for themselves. After they can't catch it, they learn to stalk, and when they stalk and stand there, real intense, we call that *a point*. He's pointing out the game . . .
>
> If you take this further, really, the bird has taught the dog to point. Because if he goes one more step, the bird's going to leave and it's all lost.
>
> BILL GIBBONS, "MAGIC MAN," *AMERICAN FIELD*,
> DECEMBER 12, 1998

UNDERSTANDING SCENT

What is your dog smelling when he scents a bird? In the bird dog world, scent refers to odors that game birds produce through their oil glands and droppings. Bird scents are carried on molecules of water that are airborne or cling to the ground or vegetation. When your pup inhales, these molecules come in contact with built-in receptors in the nasal passages of the nose. Your pup's ability to detect bird scents depends on how concentrated these odors are and how rapidly they are dispersed. Factors affecting scent include:

- weather;
- the birds' behaviors; and
- your pup's experience.

Weather includes temperature, wind, and humidity, and these conditions are constantly changing. For example, your pup may have trouble finding birds early in the morning when it is cold or the air is still. Scenting conditions usually improve as the temperatures warm or the winds pick up. Good days afield are often days with moderate humidity in the air. Low humidity can make finding birds a challenge for even the best pup.

The *birds' behaviors* can determine how much scent is available for your pup to smell. The more concentrated the scent, the longer it takes to disperse. For example, a covey of quail out feeding leaves more scent than a single bird out feeding. A single bird that flushes, lands, and sits tight will leave very little scent.

Your pup may have a good nose, but he needs *experience* to develop his nose to interpret scent. For example, he has to distinguish between birds that are present and birds that have left. He has to distinguish between live birds and wounded or dead birds. And he has to do this in constantly changing conditions while he is being bombarded with non-game scents that he must learn to ignore.

The better you understand scent, the better you appreciate

the amazing work that your pup does in pursuit of game. Just as your pup needs experience learning how to interpret scent, you also need experience learning how to interpret your pup. (For a more detailed discussion of scent, see appendix C.)

INTRODUCING GUNFIRE

If your pup is five months old, you can begin to introduce him to gunfire. Take time with this lesson and pay close attention to his initial response. When done correctly, your pup should ignore the noise. If your pup stops, changes his gait, or turns his head during the introduction, back off and give him some time to mature before continuing. Most gun-shy dogs are man-made. While some pups may be more noise-sensitive than others, a noise-sensitive pup can learn to enjoy gunfire if he is properly introduced to it.

The professionals mentioned in this book introduce gunfire in a couple of different ways. Gene Stewart likes to introduce it away from birds. This is the safest method for a beginning trainer to use. Bill Gibbons introduces gunfire around birds—when the pup makes a dive at a bird he is chasing. More-experienced trainers may prefer this method. Whichever method you choose, use a .22 caliber blank pistol or a cap gun.

Introducing Gunfire Away from Birds: GENE STEWART

Gene Stewart begins introducing gunfire while the pup is running in a field. When the pup is about five months old and confident running on different grounds, Gene shoots a blank gun when the pup is about fifty yards ahead of him. He watches to see if the pup stops or changes his gait. If he does, Gene turns and goes in a different direction, ignoring him. The pup quickly forgets about the noise and runs to catch up, but his reaction to the gunfire tells Gene that he is not ready. Gene gives him little time off, maybe a week, before trying again. Once the pup ignores the gunfire, Gene fires closer to the pup.

Introducing Gunfire:

Fire the blank gun when the pup is about fifty yards ahead.

Now, Gene is ready to introduce gunfire while the pup is looking for a bird. Gene plants a couple of quail along a tree line, as if he were introducing a pup to quail. As the pup hunts the tree line, Gene waits for him to flush a bird and chase it. When the pup chases the bird, and it lands again, he gets excited. He races around trying to find the bird, but he doesn't know where it is. At this time Gene shoots. The pup knows the bird is there, but he doesn't see or smell it.

Introducing Gunfire Around Birds:
BILL GIBBONS

Bill Gibbons likes to introduce gunfire around birds at the instant the pup makes a dive to catch the bird he is chasing.

The pup is usually so excited that he ignores the noise. Before Bill begins, he wants the pup to chase and catch a bird. Some puppies may point the bird, flush it, and aggressively chase and catch it. Other pups may be afraid of the bird, and instead of-catching it, they re-point it. A pup that re-points the bird may not be ready to fire over.

To begin the process, Bill plants a couple of pigeons with cardboard tethers in an open field as if he were introducing a pup to pigeons. He may pull some flight feathers from one wing if the bird is a strong flyer. He puts the check-cord on the pup, lets him hunt for a short time, and then brings him into a bird. The pup will either point or pounce. It doesn't matter which he does, as long as he doesn't catch the bird before it flies. Bill flushes the bird, drops the check-cord, and lets the pup chase. If the pup runs aggressively and catches the bird, he is ready to fire over.

Now, Bill works him on a second bird. He flushes the bird and lets the pup chase again. The instant the pup makes a dive for the pigeon, Bill shoots the blank pistol. He is at least fifty yards away. Bill carefully watches the pup for signs of nervousness. Did he notice the report of the gun? Most pups are so fired up from chasing birds that they ignore the noise, but once in a while a pup hesitates. If the pup hesitates at the sound of the shot, Bill works him on a third bird. This time he does not fire. He wants the pup to enjoy catching another bird before he puts him back in the kennel. Bill gives him a couple of days to think about it before reintroducing gunfire. Once the pup ignores the gunfire, Bill can shoot earlier, while the pup is chasing the bird. At this time, Bill also begins to fire multiple times and gets closer to the puppy.

Introducing the Shotgun

Once the pup is ignoring the blank gun or cap gun, he is ready to be introduced to the shotgun, but only after he has been fired over for at least a couple of weeks, and he is oblivious to the noise. A light load works best before moving to a heavy load.

Remember to introduce the larger-gauge guns in stages, the same way you introduced the blank gun.

■ ■ ■

AUTHORS' COMMENTARY

When you work your pup on birds, he learns how to use his nose. He learns:

- to be downwind to smell the bird;
- to know when the bird is there; and
- to know when the bird has gone.

Introducing your pup to birds may sound easy, but you must always be observant. Remember: If your pup acts uncertain, hesitates, or looks back at you during the introduction, his reactions are telling you that he is not yet ready for bird work. Give him a week before trying it again.

You also need to be observant when you introduce gunfire. Once successfully introduced, you must continue to be careful when you shoot. You can make your dog gun-shy at any time. Here are a few common sense rules that you should observe throughout your dog's hunting career:

- Never take your pup to a skeet or trap range to see if he is gun-shy. You could have a gun-shy pup as a result of this type of noise exposure.
- Never fire a shotgun behind your dog if he is young or inexperienced. Fire when you're in front of him so that the noise doesn't startle him.
- Use one gunner, especially for the first season. Four or five people shooting over your dog is the fastest way to send him fleeing back to the truck, panic-stricken.

- Shoot only at the birds that your dog points. If he is pointing, he is anticipating the shot. If you shoot at wild flushing birds, the noise frighten him.

As your pup's training progresses, the noise of gunfire becomes a reward. The sound tells him that birds are in the air. If you are careful, introduce the gun intelligently, and if you use common sense, your pup will thrill to the sound of the shot for the rest of his life.

■ ■ ■

TEACH WHAT'S MOST IMPORTANT FIRST.

DAVE WALKER

CHAPTER FOUR

Training During the First Eighteen Months

To be a successful hunting or field trial dog, your Brittany should be introduced to many of the situations that he will encounter as an adult dog, and he should begin to learn that the two of you are a team. In this chapter you will learn which activities to introduce to your pup and how to build teamwork. During the first eighteen months, you should:

- expose your hunting pup to early field experiences and hunt him the first season;
- build your dog's sense of dependence on you;
- expose your field trial pup to horses, the stakeout chain, "your song" (how you keep in contact with your dog), and the whistle;
- attend a field trial;
- teach him a pattern on foot or on horseback; and
- condition him to perform in the field.

TRAINING YOUR HUNTING PUP

If you plan to hunt your pup, run him in the type of cover that you will hunt. Teach him to be forward (in front of you). Encourage him to depend on you so that he is ready to go hunting the first season.

Providing Field Experience

You can begin training your pup within the first couple of weeks. Begin by getting him accustomed to the cover he will be hunting. For instance, if you live in Pennsylvania and you hunt grouse or woodcock, take him for short walks in the woods. Keep these sessions short with a young pup, as he is just starting to feel comfortable in the hunting environment.

As he explores the terrain—climbing over logs or busting through brush—teach him to be forward by walking slowly behind him and letting him lead the way. A hunting dog should work in front of you, and with these little walks you are beginning to teach him a pattern—a specific way of hunting the terrain. He may not know *where* to go yet, but he learns to be in front of you, and that the direction your body faces is the direction that you want him to go. As he gets older he learns that he can also use the sound of your voice as a directional guide.

Building Dependence

A hunting dog should depend on you. He should want to find birds with you and for you. At the same time, he needs to have enough independence to get out there and look for birds. Before you can teach your pup to depend on you, he has to show enough independence to hunt for you. Begin to build his independence when you take him for walks by going to the same area, walking the same course, and following him. Each pup is different, so let his actions guide you. Continue to follow your pup as he learns the course.

Hiding from a Puppy:

When your pup is farther away from you than you'd like him to be, duck behind a tree or bush and hide from him.

When he gets farther away from you than you would like him to be, it is time to curb his independence. Duck behind a tree or bush and hide from him. He will come looking for you. He may even get a little frantic. This is fine. Be still. He will find you. When he finds you, pet him to show that returning to you is the correct behavior. In this way you are teaching him to depend on you. This training works best before he is five months old.

When your pup reaches the stage where he stops checking in, it is again time to curb his independence by taking him to a new area. This time, don't follow him. When he takes off in one direction, start walking in another direction. Don't call him. Now, stop and wait for him to come find you. When he finds you, praise him, and continue walking. By limiting his independence, you are teaching him that he is not hunting for himself, but for you. The two of you are a team. Again, this training works best when your pup is young.

When you take your pup to new grounds and he doesn't look for you, then you may have another problem. He may be following the scent of a deer. A pup that is tracking a deer usually runs with his nose to the ground. If you suspect this is the case, stop running him until you have dealt with the deer problem. (See chapter 6, Training with the E-Collar, Using the E-Collar for Avoidance.)

As your pup gets older, carry water if the weather is hot. Call him in and give him a drink rather than letting him find water on his own. If there is snow on the ground and he gets ice balls between his pads, call him to you and pull them out. Show him you're his best buddy, and he will want to be with you.

Each pup is different, but there may be a time when your pup no longer waits for you. He may ignore you when you call him, or he may be increasingly difficult to pick up. When you can no longer control him, it is important to stop running him. You may continue walking him on a leash or check-cord, but once he stops listening or paying attention to you, do not let him run free.

The next step is yard work. During yard work, you teach

your pup the basic "whoa," "here," and "heel" commands with the check-cord, and you introduce the e-collar. Once your dog has been taught these commands, along with the e-collar (and the check-cord and training collar), you can use the e-collar as an invisible check-cord to control and correct him when he is running free.

Taking Your Pup Hunting

Assuming that your pup has had some field training with the proper exposure to birds and gunfire, and he is biddable (meaning he wants to be obedient), then by all means, take him hunting. For the first time you might want to take him to a shooting preserve and shoot for him a few strong flying birds, like chukar. The more exposure he gets to birds, the better. Try to work your pup on game birds that are strong fliers, so he can't run them down. (Naturally, the type of birds you choose depends upon the region in which you are hunting.)

Your pup should hold point long enough for you to get close before helping you flush. To help your pup hold point, try to flush by walking in from an angle or from the front, which encourages him to stand still. Walking in next to him encourages him to go with you.

Try to shoot only the birds he points, and avoid shooting bumped birds and birds he runs over. If you intend to shoot a bird, don't shoot unless you are in front of your pup, or far enough away from him that the gunfire doesn't frighten him. Let him get the bird in his mouth so he starts to see the big picture. If he knocks a bird, just smile, and when he quits listening, it's time to quit hunting.

He should hunt by himself, and there should be only one gun. Your hunting buddies and their dogs may want to join you, but multiple gunshots and other dogs can be confusing to your pup and make him gun-shy. Take your pup hunting as often as possible the first season. This early exposure to hunting will increase his eagerness to hunt and his eagerness to hunt for you.

HUNTING SAFETY

Hunting is an American tradition, and it has been an indispensable part of the development and history of this country. Hunting teaches you to be responsible in a manner that won't jeopardize the safety of others. Hunting instills in you an appreciation for nature and wildlife and a respect for the land, birds, animals, and property of others. In addition, as a hunter, you have a joint responsibility as part of a hunting party to respect the rights of the landowner and not violate the privilege of hunting on another's property. You also have a responsibility to keep your bird dogs safe.

The following are a few general hunting safety rules to consider:

1) When you first take your pup hunting, ensure that only one gun will be used, and be sure to walk in front of your pup so that he can see you shoot; too many shots can frighten a young pup.
2) Never allow the gun, either loaded or unloaded, to point in the direction of your dog or another hunter in the group; you point only at a target or bird that you intend to shoot.
3) At all times you must know the location of your dog and hunting companions.
4) Your gun should be pointed with the barrel straight up when approaching birds that are about to be flushed.
5) Your gun must be on safety at all times until you are ready to shoot.
6) Be a sportsman and allow others in your hunting party to take the first shot at game.
7) Before going over or through a fence, either give the gun to a fellow hunter, or lay it on the ground parallel to the fence, where it can be reached after crossing the fence.
8) Be sure to keep the gun barrel free from obstructions during the hunt.

9) Be sure that your gun is unloaded before transporting it in a vehicle.
10) After the hunt, be sure to clean and oil the barrel to keep the gun in good working condition.
11) Ask permission to hunt on a landowner's property.
12) Always remember that hunting is a privilege, and this privilege should never be abused.

TRAINING YOUR FIELD TRIAL PUP

If you plan to field-trial your pup, prepare him for as many experiences as possible that he is likely to encounter. These experiences should include being around horses, being on a stakeout chain, and hearing your "song" and the sounds of your whistle. If you have never been to a field trial, you should plan to attend a local trial to learn more about field-trialing with your pup.

Learning about Horses

Contact with horses is important because judges in both walking and horseback trials are on horseback. If you don't own a horse, try to attend a "fun" trial (non-sanctioned field trial held for fun) so you can get your pup around horses. If you compete in horseback trials, get your pup around horses as soon as possible. Your pup needs to see and smell them. Use an experienced field trial horse, especially if your pup is bold, in case your pup decides to nip at him. Like introducing anything, go slowly. If your pup acts scared, back off and try again in a couple of weeks.

Introducing the Stakeout Chain

The *stakeout chain* is a safe way for you to secure one or more dogs when you are training or at a field trial. It is also called a *chain-gang* or *line*. To introduce a young pup to the stakeout chain, put him at the end of the line near a stake so that the older dogs can't jerk him around. At first he may fight the chain. Be patient. Leave him there for short periods of time. Repeat this procedure over the next couple of days until he is comfortable, and be sure to have water available for your dog at all times.

Three-Dog Stakeout

To make a stakeout chain, use a single length of chain and attach a metal ring on each end. Attach short pieces of chain (about 18 inches long) at approximately 4-foot intervals on the single length of chain and put swivel snaps on the ends of the short pieces. To hold the long chain in place, drive stakes into the ground through the rings. Then, hook the snaps to your dogs' identification collars.

"Singing" and Using a Whistle

Your dog's job is to find birds. He shouldn't hunt at your feet but should range out to hunt productive covers. When he finds birds, he should point and hold them until you get there. Sometimes your dog will be out of sight because of terrain or cover, but you need to stay in touch with him. You keep contact by "singing" to him. This "song," often based on the word *yo* (or *ho*), can be sung softly and repeated to let the dog know where you are, or it can be sung sharply, like YO! to get the dog's attention. Handlers develop unique "songs" that they sing to their dogs.

You can also use a whistle. If it is windy or if you have a soft voice, a whistle will help you stay in contact with your dog. You can also use it to release your dog or to tell him that he is doing it right. Like your voice, the type of whistle you use and the way you use it are personal decisions. Your dog soon learns to recognize your sounds as belonging to you. Choose the sounds that are comfortable to you, and be consistent.

Attending Your First Field Trial

If you have never been to a field trial, plan to attend one to watch and ask questions. You might decide that you would like to compete with your dog. There are many different organizations, including the American Kennel Club and the American Field, that sponsor field events, and the rules vary depending on which organization sponsors the trial. For more information on events in your area, contact the American Brittany Club (http://clubs.akc.org/brit).

A field trial is made up of different stakes (individual events). Each stake is defined by a dog's age and ability. Here is some information about the different types of stakes that may be offered if you plan to attend an AKC walking or horseback field trial.

- To compete in a puppy stake, a puppy must be between six and fifteen months old. If a puppy has game contact, the handler may be required to fire a blank gun. Puppies run for at least fifteen minutes, but no more than thirty minutes.
- To compete in a derby stake, a derby dog must be between six months to two years old. A derby dog must establish point. If handlers are within gun range, they must fire a blank gun. Derby dogs run for twenty to thirty minutes.
- To compete in a gun dog stake, a dog has to be at least six months old, be steady-to-wing-and-shot, and back (honor another dog's point) if the opportunity presents itself. Gun dogs run for at least thirty minutes.
- An all-age stake is the same as a gun dog stake,

but an all-age dog must show more independence and hunt beyond gun range.

Each stake is made up of braces. A *brace* is a pair of dogs that run together. The number of braces depends on the number of entries. If twenty dogs are entered in a gun dog stake, there are ten gun dog braces. A running order is determined by a drawing and is printed up before the day of the trial.

When it is time for a specific brace to run, the two handlers take their dogs to the line on leads and break them away (release the dogs). A thirty-minute course can cover two to three miles of ground. The handlers walk or ride behind the dogs and try to keep them on course by singing and using their whistles. Two judges, one for each handler, follow. Two scouts, one for each handler, look for the dogs if they get off course or are ridden past where they are on point. The scouts must stay behind the judges. The *gallery*—which is made up of people on foot or horseback—follows, and must also stay behind the judges. At a weekend trial the gallery may have twenty to thirty people in it, while at a national championship, the gallery may number in the hundreds.

Quail or other game birds have been released on the course, and the dogs have to find and point them. Dogs are judged on their desire to hunt, on the way they cover the ground, and on their manners. The dog that comes closest to the standard for each stake wins. Winning dogs receive points toward their field championships, and winning handlers receive ribbons and trophies.

Field trials are competitive events, but they are also social events for dogs and handlers. Dogs enjoy the friendly atmosphere and interact with other dogs and people on a variety of grounds. Handlers are competitive, but this competitive spirit does not interfere with the sportsmanship and the fellowship that are integral elements of the sport. Since field events are held throughout the year, they provide a way of enjoying hunting with your dog year-round and sharing the camaraderie that comes with the sport.

Teaching a Pattern:
TOMMY TRACY

When a dog is taught where to run, he is taught a pattern—a specific way of hunting the terrain. *Being forward* (in front of you) is one of the first patterns that he learns. *Running an edge* (such as a tree line, ravine, and so forth) or *running to certain objectives* (places that may hold birds) are examples of more-advanced patterns. The patterns you teach your dog will depend on the types of terrain and birds that you hunt. In this section Tommy Tracy's methods for developing a dog's pattern for handlers on foot and for handlers on horseback are discussed (the latter in detail).

Tommy uses a beeper collar and a cable—two important pieces of equipment—to teach a pattern. A *beeper collar* emits a beeping sound to locate a dog when he is out of sight or when he is on point. A *cable* slows a dog down so that he doesn't get too far ahead of his handler. Both a beeper collar and a cable should be introduced to a dog before they are used in training. Tommy introduces the beeper collar first. When the dog is ready for the cable, Tommy puts the e-collar on him, but he doesn't turn it on. (Discussion of the e-collar is included in chapter 6.)

INTRODUCING THE BEEPER COLLAR

Tommy introduces the beeper collar in stages so that the pup isn't afraid of it. He turns the beeper collar on and hangs it somewhere near the kennel to get the pup accustomed to the noise. Tommy also runs the pup with the beeper collar before turning it on to get him accustomed to wearing it.

When the pup ignores the noise of the beeper

collar in the kennel, Tommy turns it on when he takes him for a run. If the pup acts frightened, Tommy turns the sound off but continues to run him with the beeper collar on his neck. Tommy continues to hang the beeper collar near the pup's kennel and reintroduces it in the field in a couple of days. Eventually, the pup gets excited when he hears the beeping noise because he recognizes it as a signal that lets him know he is going to have fun.

Dog in a Roading Harness Dragging a Cable:

This dog is dragging a cable that is attached to the roading harness that he is wearing. Notice he is also wearing an e-collar and beeper.

INTRODUCING THE CABLE

When the dog starts running so fast that Tommy can't keep up with him, the dog is ready for the cable. Tommy attaches the cable to the center ring of the roading harness, which slows the dog down enough so that Tommy can keep up with him, whether on foot or on horseback. The cable controls the range and speed of the dog so that Tommy doesn't have to do so.

The cable is made of welding cable. The black rubber coating is smooth and stiff and doesn't get tangled. Tommy uses different lengths and diameters according to the size of the dog and the condition of the terrain. As the length and the diameter increase, the cable gets heavier. In addition to the actual weight of the cable, it also has a drag weight. A light cable that is very long may be harder to pull than a heavier cable that is short. Conditions can affect drag. Higher cover or dry (as opposed to wet) ground can make the cable harder to pull. To make a good all-around cable for a Brittany, Tommy uses an 8- to 10-foot piece of MIG cable (three copper wires), weighing about 3 pounds, and uses duct tape to attach a swivel snap at one end.

Tommy introduces the cable in stages before the dog runs with it. When Tommy begins to have trouble keeping up with the dog, he puts the dog in a roading harness and attaches a check-cord. Once the dog is comfortable dragging the check-cord, Tommy switches to a light cable before going to a heavier one. An older dog may not like the cable if he hasn't been run with one before. He may stop and refuse to run. For a dog like this, Tommy does not take the cable off, and eventually, the dog gives in and runs again.

Patterning on Foot

Developing a pattern on foot is difficult. Staying ahead of your pup to avoid his "looping" back to you is vital. The following step-by-step process for teaching your pup a pattern is based on the method Tommy uses:

- Release your pup with a blast of your whistle.
- Move ahead. If your pup stops, speed up.
- If your pup putters around, leave him.
- Once your pup understands that he is to work in front of you, move to the side when he takes an edge.
- If your pup breaks off the edge and comes

toward you, run toward him, cutting him off and forcing him to turn back toward the edge.

- The instant your pup turns, blow your whistle to let him know that is what you want him to do. When your pup is back on the edge, blow the whistle again and sing to him to tell him he is doing it right.
- Soon your pup learns that your song tells him where you are and what you want him to do. He doesn't have to see you.
- When your pup checks in, looking for direction, move in the direction you want him to go.

To more thoroughly understand the process of teaching your dog a pattern, study the following detailed explanation of the method Tommy uses to teach a pattern from horseback.

Patterning on Horseback

Tommy runs a pup from horseback when the pup is at least six months old and has already been introduced to horses. The first step is teaching the pup to be forward. To begin the process, Tommy blows the whistle to release the pup. Initially, the whistle blast means nothing to the pup, but, with repetition, the pup learns that Tommy wants him to "go." The pup doesn't know where to go, but Tommy rides slowly and follows him. If the pup putters or gets behind, Tommy doesn't slow down; he speeds up. The pup thinks he is being left behind and hurries to catch up.

Once the pup understands that he is to be in front of the horse, he begins to learn that the direction Tommy's horse is headed is the direction that Tommy wants him to go. Now, Tommy is ready to teach him to run an edge such as a tree line. Tommy rides to one side of the pup—not directly behind him. Thus, when the pup is on an edge, Tommy is out in the field. If the pup comes off the edge, Tommy is out in the field and in position to redirect the pup to the edge. Tommy rides diagonally toward the edge so that the pup has to turn or run into the horse. Tommy blows the whistle the instant the pup turns. The whistle blast lets the pup know that he is doing it right. When the pup gets back on the edge, Tommy blows the whistle again to let him know that he did the right thing. This is the way Tommy introduces the whistle.

Along with using the whistle, Tommy sings to the pup. Like the whistle, he uses his song to tell the pup when he is doing something right or when he is doing something wrong. Tommy uses a low voice to tell pup he is doing it right. If his voice changes or if it raises an octave, the pup is doing something wrong. The longer the pup continues doing something incorrectly, such as turning the wrong way, running in the wrong direction, and so forth, the higher Tommy's voice gets. The change in his voice gets the pup's attention, and, once the pup corrects himself, Tommy returns to using a lower voice to give a signal to the pup that his behavior is appropriate.

Each pup has a space between him and his handler with which he is comfortable. As Tommy and the pup continue the process, Tommy watches the pup to see where his comfort zone is—every pup is different—and then uses this space to help teach the pup to stay on an edge. Tommy knows that if he gets too close to the pup, the pup will move farther away from him (come off the edge) to maintain his comfort zone. He also knows that if he gets too far away from the pup, the pup will move closer to him (come off the edge) to maintain his comfort zone.

Initially, Tommy runs a young pup in the middle of the day when quail aren't out feeding so that the pup concentrates on him. When the pup gets the idea that Tommy wants him to stay on an edge, Tommy is ready to put birds there for him to find. When the pup finds birds on the edge, running an edge makes sense to him because the edge is where the birds are.

The pup is becoming more independent and runs faster and farther out, and Tommy has introduced the beeper collar. When Tommy has to keep his horse in a lope, it is time to slow the pup down. Tommy prepares the pup for the cable by putting a roading harness on him and attaching a check-cord. Tommy also puts the e-collar on him, but he doesn't turn it on. The pup quickly forgets about the added gear because he is having so much fun hunting, and, after a couple of training sessions, he thinks of the gear as part of his uniform. Eventually, Tommy uses the e-collar—along with his voice, whistle, and cable—to control the dog.

In this phase of the training, the pup is dragging the cable. Tommy has been building his independence, and he takes an edge without Tommy's help. Up until now Tommy ran him on the same course the same way and followed him. At a certain point, the pup runs the course because he knows it, not because Tommy asks him to do it. Once the pup stops paying attention to Tommy, Tommy changes the course. If the pup goes one way, Tommy makes him go another way. Now the pup isn't sure where to go, so he has to depend on Tommy again. By making the pup more dependent on him, Tommy is teaching the pup that they are a team. The pup is learning to go where Tommy tells him to go—not where he wants to go.

CONDITIONING

The Brittany is a bird dog and an athlete. In order to perform in the field—whether hunting or field trials—a Brittany must be in excellent physical shape. Too often people expect their dogs to hunt half a day in temperatures that exceed 70 degrees Fahrenheit. Do not hunt your dog in such weather unless he has been conditioned. If your dog is out of shape, begin to gradually condition him, and don't have unrealistic expectations for an older dog.

In conditioning your dog, you must learn to "read" him, to be sensitive to his needs. Being aware of your dog's needs is most important during hot weather. Be sure that you water him early and often. Depending on the weather conditions of your area, you may want to use electric clippers to shave his coat, or you may take him to a dog grooming shop and ask that he be given a "field cut"—a short cut appropriate to the weather conditions of the area.

Conditioning the Hunting Dog: GENE STEWART

To hunt birds, a hunting dog needs to be able to work in the uplands for several hours at a time. During the summer months before the fall bird season, Gene says that the best way to condition a dog is to "road" him—letting him pull in a harness that is attached to a moving vehicle (such as an ATV, bicycle, sled, and so forth) or to a horse. When Gene roads a dog, he starts with ten- to fifteen-minute sessions, twice a week. At regular intervals he increases the conditioning sessions to every other day. Gradually, he increases the length of the sessions to thirty or forty minutes.

If you do not have a vehicle or horse for roading your dog, you can condition him by walking him in a roading harness on a check-cord and attaching a length of chain or cable to the roading harness. Use a chain only when you are roading on a smooth surface, such as level ground or a paved area. The chain should weigh about 5 pounds, and the cable should weigh about 3 pounds and be 8 to 10 feet long. Because this additional weight increases the stress on your dog, you should reduce the time of the workout by one-half.

Conditioning the Field Trial Dog: TOMMY TRACY

Tommy says that using the roading harness and cable are essential to the proper conditioning of a field trial dog. When he first starts a dog on a conditioning program, Tommy roads the dog with an ATV or with a horse, for two short periods of time—five to ten minutes—every other day. He believes that it is important to vary these two times during the day—early morning and late evening one day, and midmorning and early afternoon the next day.

If you do not have an ATV or a horse, Tommy suggests, as does Gene Stewart, that you use cables for conditioning. He recommends using two cables, one on each side of the dog. In this way the muscles on both sides of the dog are equally conditioned. He also says that instead of walking, you can ride a bicycle to road him.

When preparing for a field trial, depending on weather conditions, Tommy suggests using the following conditioning process:

- Road from one to one and a half hours every other day.
- Vary the time of day for roading.
- Lay up (stop conditioning) two days before the trial.
- When conditioning in the summer, do not overdo it. Vary the conditioning with the temperature, and do less conditioning during extremely hot weather.
- When you first start roading your dog, give him water within the first ten minutes. Subsequently, give him water as needed.

AUTHORS' COMMENTARY

Each pup is unique, and although you can't change his basic nature, you can modify his behavior through training. A hunting dog should be dependent. If your hunting pup becomes too independent, you can hide from him or take him to new grounds. A field trial pup should be more independent. You can build your pup's independence by running him on familiar grounds and following him. You teach teamwork to both types of puppies by encouraging them to depend on you and by varying the amount of dependency to fit your needs.

Prepare your pup for success by introducing him to

the activities that he will participate in as an adult. Some of the activities may differ for the hunting pup and the field trial pup, but both types of pups should feel comfortable in their surroundings. The hunting pup must learn to bust through brush, and the field trial pup must get accustomed to being around horses. The sound of the beeper collar should excite both types of pups, and they should enjoy pulling the cable or roading in a harness. Remember to pay close attention to your pup's reactions. If you don't skip steps or move him along faster than he is able to go when you are training him, you will have a happy dog—one that enjoys his work and brings you pleasure.

PUSHING A DOG FASTER THAN HE CAN GO IS THE SLOWEST WAY TO GET THERE.

BILL GIBBONS

CHAPTER FIVE

Beginning Yard Work

In this book, *yard work* refers to the training that takes place when your Brittany is restrained with a check-cord or controlled with an e-collar in a "training field" or "yard." The information in this chapter focuses on how to use the check-cord to teach your dog the three basic commands: "whoa," "here," and "heel." Your dog also wears a training collar and an e-collar, although the e-collar is not used until your dog learns the commands.

Yard work firmly establishes who the boss is. Do not teach these commands until you can enforce them with the e-collar. If your dog learns to ignore your commands, he will never respect your authority. As yard work progresses, you introduce the e-collar to your dog and use it to correct him each time he disobeys a command that you have already taught him. Eventually, the e-collar becomes an invisible check-cord that controls your dog as he works farther and farther away from you. (The e-collar is discussed in detail in chapter 6, Training with the E-Collar.)

The Training Collar

THE TRAINING COLLAR

There are different styles and types of training collars. Dave Walker and Bill Gibbons use special leather collars of their own designs that have a row of flat rivets along the inside. The check-cord attaches to a ring at the end of the training collar.

Your dog should be accustomed to wearing a training collar before training begins. If the training collar frightens your dog, Dave Walker and Bill Gibbons recommend unhooking the check-cord from the training collar, attaching it to your dog's identification collar, and leaving the training collar in place. These training collars do not cause pain or injury to your dog. They help get your dog's attention. Your dog also learns that when he is wearing the training collar, he is expected to work and not play.

THE CHECK-CORD

The check-cord referred to in this book is a stiff rope that won't tangle in the brush. It is about 1/2 inch in diameter, is comfortable to hold, and is about 12 feet long, with a swivel snap at one end. It is the least expensive and most important piece of dog training equipment you will own.

There is a specific way to handle the check-cord in order to train your dog. In this book, the term tug—as in "the tug of the check-cord"—describes the action that the trainer makes with the check-cord. Different trainers describe this action differently, but the principle is the same. Dave Walker calls it a "quick flip of the wrist." Bill Gibbons describes it as a "light little jerk you can barely see." While the description is not important, the action is. The tug is a momentary action followed by an immediate release—not constant pressure.

Your dog has to be comfortable walking on the check-cord before he is ready to learn commands. He has to understand that when he pulls against the check-cord, he is applying pressure against himself. He also should be able to untangle himself if the rope gets wrapped around him. in "the tug of the check-cord"—describes the action.

Teaching "Whoa": DAVE WALKER

Whoa means to "stop and stand still" until released. It is used to stop your dog in the field and is the most important command your dog will learn. Dave first teaches "whoa" as a nonverbal command. He uses a quick tug of the check-cord to teach the dog to stop and stand still and to let him walk in front of the dog. He then releases the dog with a tap on the side. The process of teaching the nonverbal "whoa" command takes a week or more, although some dogs catch on faster than others. Dave introduces the verbal "whoa" once the dog has learned the silent command.

To begin, Dave puts the training collar below the identification collar. He puts the e-collar above the identification collar—even if he doesn't plan to use it—and he attaches the check-cord to the training collar.

Positioning the Training Collar

E-collar

Identification collar

Put the training collar below the dog's identification collar.

Dave starts by walking the dog in his training field, and he teaches him to walk on the loose check-cord—and, most important, to walk without pulling. The dog has to learn not to pull because, eventually, he will have the opportunity to point birds, and he cannot establish point if he is pulling. To teach the dog not to pull, Dave gives him a couple of quick tugs (a flip of the wrist) with the check-cord. If he ignores the tugs and continues to pull, Dave gently spins the dog.

The trainer holds the end of the training collar (near the ring) in both hands and lifts the dog up so that he is standingon his hind legs. Slowly he spins the dog in a circle. The faster he spins him, the stronger the correction. Spinning doesn't hurt the dog, but it does disorient him. One or two spins are usually enough to settle the dog down so that training can continue.

Spinning the Dog

Once the dog is walking on the loose check-cord at Dave's side, Dave stops the dog with a quick tug of the check-cord. He may need to give a couple of tugs to get him to stand still. When he stands still, Dave shows the dog his approval by petting him. With a couple of long soft strokes of his hand, Dave pushes down gently, applying pressure on the withers and the hips as his hand glides from the head to the tail. Because dogs instinctively resist pressure by pushing back, the dog reacts to the pressure being applied to his withers and hips by pushing back—making him stand taller. While Dave strokes the dog, he holds his head still with the other hand. Dave wants to prevent the dog from looking around. A dog that is looking around isn't paying attention. Dave taps the dog on the side to release him and continues walking. He tugs the check-cord and stops the dog a few more times. Next, he tries to get out in front of the dog. Eventually, when Dave tugs the check-cord, the dog stops and stands still and lets Dave walk in front and pretend to flush.

Stroking a Dog

While the trainer strokes the dog, he holds the head still with the other hand.

Up to this point, Dave has not spoken the word *Whoa*. Once the dog stops when Dave tugs the check-cord, stands still while he walks in front of him, kicks around, throws his hat, and so forth—pretending to flush—he is then ready to introduce the verbal "whoa." Dave continues to walk him around the training field, but this time, at the instant he tugs the check-cord, he says, "Whoa." It only takes a few times before the dog is stopping when Dave says this command.

Dave is quiet during yard work. He never speaks to the dog except to give him commands. He uses the check-cord and his body language to communicate with the dog and teach him the basic commands. When the dog does well, Dave praises him by petting him. When the dog makes a mistake, he corrects him with a quick tug of the check-cord or spins him in a circle with the training collar for a stronger correction.

Teaching "Here": DAVE WALKER

Here has two meanings in yard work—"go with me" and "come to me."

Go with Me Dave first introduces the "here" command to mean "go with me." He lays the groundwork for the "here" command at the same time he is working the dog on "stop and stand still." As Dave walks the dog on the check-cord, he turns and begins to walk in a different direction. At the exact moment when he turns, he lightly tugs the check-cord and says, "Here." The dog looks up, sees Dave going in a new direction, and swings around with him. Dave is teaching the dog that "here" and a tug of the check-cord mean "go with me." Dave says it is important for him to be turned in a new direction before he tugs the check-cord. He wants the dog to see that he has turned when he says, "Here." The dog naturally wants to turn and go with him. When Dave turns, the dog is learning to swing around with him. Understanding and obeying this command is essential to both working the dog on foot or off horseback.

Come to Me Once the dog understands that he is to go with Dave when he hears the command, Dave occasionally stops and says "Here." When he calls the dog to him, he faces the dog. If the dog doesn't respond, Dave coaxes him with little tugs of the check-cord. Dogs understand body language and have no trouble sorting out the two meanings of this command.

Combining "Whoa" and "Here": DAVE WALKER

As the training progresses, Dave drops the check-cord and lets the dog drag it. He gives the command "Whoa," and the dog stops. He walks over to the dog and shows his approval by stroking him. Then he gets out in front of the dog, pretends to flush, throws his hat, walks back to the dog, strokes him again, and taps him on the side to release him. Dave changes direction, gives the command "Here," and the dog goes with him. Dave calls "Here," faces the dog, and the dog comes to him.

Teaching "Heel": BEN LORENSON

Some dogs learn to heel as they are being taught to walk on a loose lead, but other dogs want to forge ahead. To teach a dog to walk at his side, Ben uses the check-cord.

Ben taps his thigh with his hand to get the dog's attention. He is signaling to the dog that he wants him to walk next to his thigh, at his heel. If the dog gets out of the heel position, Ben quickly tugs and releases the check-cord a couple of times. Once the dog is back in position, Ben continues to walk with the loose check-cord. If the dog gets ahead or behind, he gives a few quick tugs of the check-cord until the dog walks next to his thigh.

To reinforce the lesson, Ben takes the end of the check-cord and holds it about three feet from the end and rapidly twirls the loose end in a vertical circle in front of him. If the dog moves in front of Ben, he walks into the twirling check-cord. This is his choice, and he can back out real fast. After walking into the twirling check-cord a couple of times, the dog quickly learns that he is supposed to walk *beside* Ben, not in front of him.

Barrel Training:
TOMMY TRACY

Barrel training helps teach your dog to stand still. It also helps develop your dog's balance, composure, and patience. Tommy begins barrel training as soon as he gets a new dog. The dog might be as young as five months or as old as two years. Older dogs need more time to master the barrel, but they can also benefit from it.

Tommy begins by placing the dog on a fifty-five-gallon plastic drum that has been turned on its side and placed on a wooden pallet—so it doesn't roll—conveniently located to one side of his kennel. Tommy gently lifts the dog onto the barrel. He doesn't say anything. He just pets the dog under the chin and strokes his tail to style him up, posing him in a pointing position. Tommy is teaching the dog to stand still. If the dog comes off the barrel, Tommy carefully puts him back on the barrel; dogs don't like to come off the barrel and hit the ground, so they try harder to stay on it. After a couple of sessions, he begins to stand on the barrel for longer periods of time.

AUTHORS' COMMENTARY

When you begin yard work, start out slowly and don't expect to see immediate results. Your dog has to respond to the "whoa" and "here" commands in conjunction with the check-cord before he is ready to learn the e-collar. He may appear to grasp something one day, only to not get it the next day. Begin each session with a review. If he has trouble understanding something new, go back to something he can handle successfully and finish on a positive note. Dog training takes patience, and not every training session goes smoothly. If you lose your temper or get frustrated, stop training so that you don't take your feelings out on your dog. It is better to wait and train another day.

Continue doing yard work throughout your dog's career. During the hunting or field trial season, your dog may forget some of these lessons. When this happens, bring him back to the "yard" for a tune-up. You may decide to teach him to be steady-to-wing-and-shot or to undertake additional training such as stop-to-flush, backing, and retrieving. Be sure that you understand how to teach the basic commands before you move with your dog to the next level of training.

■ ■ ■

A LITTLE BIT AT A TIME
IS BETTER THAN ALL AT ONCE.

TOMMY TRACY

CHAPTER SIX

Training with the E-Collar

The electronic collar (or e-collar) is an extremely important training tool. Although there are many different ways for trainers to introduce and use the e-collar, methods discussed in this book are those proven to be most effective for training Brittanys. The e-collar has three functions:

- making corrections—correcting your dog when he makes a mistake for something he has already learned;
- gaining attention—getting your dog's attention; and
- teaching avoidance—ignoring non-game species such as deer, snakes, and so forth.

The e-collar is a sophisticated electrical training device that bears little resemblance to the shock collars of yesteryear. It can be adjusted and fine-tuned to fit the sensitivity of individual dogs, and it can be used in a variety of situations. Generally, it is introduced in yard work with the check-cord and the training collar. As training progresses, the e-collar is used to control the dog once he is running without the check-cord. This entire chapter is devoted to the e-collar because it is such an important training tool.

PRESENTING THE E-COLLAR

When your pup is about five or six months old, you can begin putting the e-collar on him. You won't turn it on right away, but your dog should wear it every time he goes afield. Get him accustomed to running with it so he thinks that it is part of his uniform. You may be surprised at how excited he gets when you put it on him.

If your dog is older, be sure that he wears the e-collar for at least a month before you turn it on. Your dog can become "collar-wise" if you put the e-collar on him, turn it on, and immediately start using it. A collar-wise dog learns to obey commands only when he is wearing the e-collar. To avoid having a collar-wise dog, introduce the e-collar slowly and always have him wear it in the field, no matter how old or well trained he is.

THE E-COLLAR

The e-collar referred to in this book is the Tri-Tronics Pro 200. This e-collar has two parts: the collar (receiver) that the dog wears and the transmitter that the trainer carries. The transmitter has two black buttons – one for low, second for medium momentary stimulation. When both buttons are pressed together, high momentary stimulation is achieved. The red button is for continuous stimulation. It also has a selection switch for five intensity levels. Momentary stimulation is a preset amount of stimulation that is delivered regardless of how long the button is held down. Continuous stimulation is stimulation that is delivered as long as the button is held down—a maximum of nine seconds. Amateurs probably should use momentary stimulation for most of their training. They make fewer mistakes since it is preset and shuts off automatically. The continuous button is used for avoidance training.

The transmitter can be carried in a hunting vest or holster. Different holster styles attach to a belt, shoulder strap, or saddle.

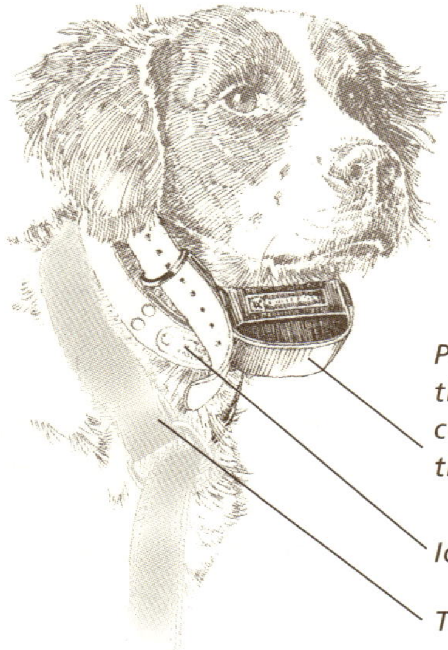

Positioning the E-Collar:

Put the e-collar above the dog's identification collar with the probes on the underside of the neck.

Identification collar

Training collar

Fitting the E-Collar on Your Dog

Position the e-collar above your dog's identification collar with the probes on the underside of the neck. This position is closest to the ears, which is the narrowest part of the neck. Placed in this position, it can't slide around. The e-collar needs to be snug enough so that the probes are always in contact with your dog's neck as he runs, but not so tight that it chokes him. If the e-collar is too loose, you may erroneously think that the level of stimulation is too low because your dog is not responding to the stimulation. Actually, your dog is not responding to the stimulation because he is not receiving it.

Finding Your Dog's Level

If you have never used an e-collar, determining the level of intensity can be tricky. Each dog is different. Brittanys usually aren't tough dogs, so it is better to begin with too little stimulation than to begin with too much. If you have five levels of momentary stimulation on the transmitter, begin with the first level. Your dog's response should be subtle—indicated by a muscle twitch in the neck or shoulder or by a turning of the head. If he yelps or shakes his head, the setting is too high. The e-collar is a great training tool, but you must use it carefully, with know-how gained from experience in the field. If you have never used an e-collar or are unsure about using one, ask someone who is proficient with it to help you. If you don't know anyone to advise you, get a videotape that explains the use of this device. (For further information, see appendix A.)

It is very important to test the e-collar on yourself. You must know what your dog is feeling. Start with the first level. Place the points on the palm of your hand or your arm. Feel the stimulation on all three buttons. Next, move up to the second level and feel the difference. It is a good idea to periodically check the stimulation on your hand or arm to be sure that the e-collar is functioning properly.

Using the Transmitter

Different pros have different descriptions of the way they press the buttons on the transmitter. Bill Gibbons likens himself to a woodpecker pecking away at the buttons. Ben Lorenson talks about developing a touch or a feel for the e-collar. He says that this happens once the trainer learns how to use the e-collar to communicate with the dog.

However you describe it, the pros press the transmitter buttons often and use low levels of stimulation. As you become comfortable with the e-collar, try to use it like the pros do—at lower levels for correction and attention. If you only use the e-collar at higher levels for major corrections and avoidance training, neither you nor your dog will reap the benefits that come from using this device.

USING THE E-COLLAR FOR CORRECTION

The most important use of the e-collar is to correct your dog. If you have bought an e-collar, you probably already know this, but your dog doesn't. Your job is to teach him that the stimulation is a result of his actions. You introduce the e-collar by showing him that the e-collar is the same as the tug of the check-cord. Some dogs catch on more quickly than others, but it takes about a month of training before a dog begins to understand that the stimulation is the result of his behavior, and if he changes his behavior, the stimulation stops.

Introducing the E-Collar for the First Time: BILL GIBBONS

Bill uses the leather training collar and check-cord to introduce the e-collar for the first time. The dog has to have enough yard work training to be able to walk on the loose check-cord and "stop and stand still" when Bill tugs the check-cord. With the e-collar on the dog's neck and the check-cord attached to the training collar, Bill starts walking the dog. For review, Bill tugs the check-cord, and the dog stops. He pets the dog for standing and then taps the dog on the side to release him and continues walking. As the dog is walking, Bill gives a soft tug that he knows the dog will ignore. In one hand Bill holds the check-cord and in the other one he holds the transmitter. The instant that the dog ignores the tug, Bill touches him with low stimulation. The dog should stop. If he doesn't, Bill again tugs the check-cord to stop him. Once the dog stops, Bill pets him, taps him on the side to release him, and continues. Bill gives another soft tug with the check-cord that he thinks the dog will ignore. When the dog ignores it, Bill touches him again with low stimulation. This time he may touch the same button a couple of times in a row. If the dog doesn't stop, Bill tugs the check-cord again to stop him. Bill is teaching the dog that the stimulation is the result of his not stopping. It is the same as the tug of the check-cord.

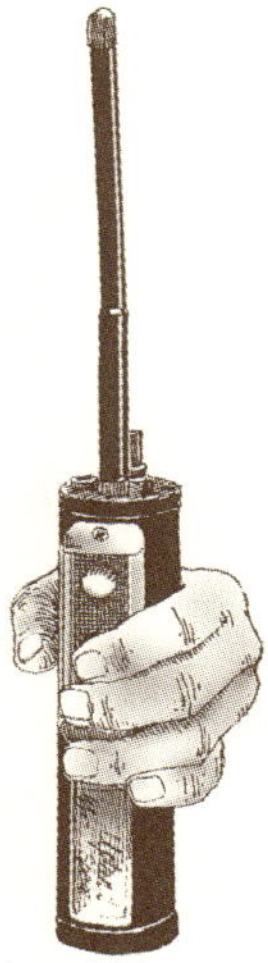

Hand Resting on the transmitter

His hand resting on the transmitter, the trainer is ready to instantly deliver the stimulation to make the correction.

Timing is everything, so Bill's hand rests on the transmitter. He is ready to deliver the stimulation to make the correction the instant that the dog makes a mistake. If Bill is unable to deliver the stimulation immediately, he does not deliver it but waits for the next opportunity. Correcting the dog after the fact only confuses him.

Bill continues to work the dog in short sessions, three times a week, until the dog is stopping on his own when he feels the stimulation. Bill increases the level of stimulation if he gets no response after he hits the same button two or three times.

Doing Yard Work with the E-Collar

Once you have introduced the e-collar, continue to use it in yard work. At first your dog may not realize what the stimulation means, so you help him understand that the stimulation is a correction by working him on commands that he already knows.

Work him on "whoa" using a tug of the check-cord, or say "Whoa." If your dog doesn't stop, correct him with the check-cord or with the e-collar, alternating between the two. When you use the e-collar, use the least amount of stimulation to get the desired response. When he stops, stroke him for standing and release him with a tap on the side. You are teaching him that the stimulation is a correction for not stopping.

For the "here" command, turn your body and say "Here." If your dog doesn't turn, alternate between correcting him with a tug of the check-cord or stimulation. Occasionally, turn toward him and call him to you. Correct him with the check-cord or stimulation if he doesn't respond. You are teaching him that the stimulation is a correction for not "going with you" or not "coming to you." At this level you continue to hold the check-cord and use it to help him remember the commands if he becomes confused.

Understanding the Stimulation: BEN LORENSON

The next step is to drop the check-cord and let the dog drag it. At this level of training, you use the stimulation—by itself—to correct the dog. The dog must understand that the stimulation is a correction for his behavior, and he must understand "whoa" and "here." To determine if he is ready to drag the check-cord, Ben gives him a test on the "whoa" and "here" commands. Ben wants the dog to ignore these commands so that he can use the stimulation to correct him. How the dog reacts to the stimulation tells Ben if he understands that the stimulation is a correction.

To begin, Ben walks the dog on the check-cord and says "Whoa." The dog stops. Ben walks in front of the dog and tries to pull the dog toward him with a couple of gentle tugs. If the dog starts to come to him, Ben touches him with low stimulation for moving. The dog stops. Ben walks back to the dog, taps him on the side to release him, and continues to walk him. Ben stops him again by saying "Whoa". He gets out in front of the dog and tries to pull the dog toward him again. If the dog moves, Ben touches him with low stimulation. Now the dog is standing still. Ben says "Here," and calls the dog to him. At this point he may not want to move. Ben gives a gentle tug on the check-cord and repeats "Here." If the dog ignores the command, Ben touches him with low stimulation. If he doesn't respond to the stimulation by coming, he is letting Ben know that he doesn't understand the correction. If the dog comes, he is telling Ben that he is ready to advance to the next level of training. Now Ben can drop the check-cord and let him drag it.

Testing a Dog's Comprehension of "Whoa".

The trainer tries to pull the dog toward him with a couple of gentle tugs.

At this level in training, stimulation is making the dog think about what he is doing. If the dog seems confused at any time, Ben goes back to holding the check-cord and reviews the basics. Some dogs take longer to catch on than others, but the dog can't advance to the next phase of training until he gives the right response to the e-collar corrections.

Using Two E-Collars:
GENE STEWART

Putting the e-collar on different parts of a dog's body is another technique to help a dog understand stimulation. Gene puts the e-collar on the dog's belly to introduce stimulation and enforce the "whoa" command because the dog's reaction is to stop when he feels stimulation on his belly. You should have experience with the e-collar before using this method.

Instead of introducing the "whoa" command and the e-collar with the check-cord on the dog's neck, Gene attaches the check-cord to the identification collar and wraps it around the dog's belly to form a half hitch. If he tugs the check-cord, the point of contact is on the dog's belly and not his neck. Gene holds the end of the check-cord and walks the dog in the half hitch until he relaxes. Once the dog is relaxed Gene puts the e-collar around the belly. The probes are underneath. The e-collar has to be tight enough for the points to make contact but loose enough that the dog can run. Initially, the dog may run with a cock-eyed gait, but his gait should smooth out once he becomes accustomed to wearing it. Gene runs the dog with the e-collar for about a month before using it.

Gene uses the check-cord and half hitch to teach the "whoa" command and introduce stimulation. Once the dog is stopping when he feels the stimulation on the belly, Gene is ready to introduce the "here" command. He puts a second e-collar on the dog's neck. Gene has one transmitter that operates both e-collars. When the dog feels the stimulation on the neck, his reaction is to turn his head away from the stimulation. As Gene walks the dog on the check-cord, he turns, says "Here," and touches him with low stimulation. The dog turns his head, sees Gene, and swings around with him.

Gene continues to use the half hitch and the e-collar on the belly to teach and enforce the "whoa" command, as well as to introduce the dog to birds. He wants the dog to associate stimulation on the belly with the "whoa" command and with birds. He continues to use the e-collar on the neck for the "here" commands.

Training Tips

- Never use the e-collar to correct your dog if you can't see him. He may be standing on point.
- It is better to correct your dog with low stimulation multiple times than to touch him with low stimulation one time and, if there is no response, go immediately to the next level.
- If the low and medium buttons don't give you a response, and you are using the high button most of the time, move up to the next intensity level. When your dog responds to the higher intensity level, you may be able to drop down a level for the next correction because your dog remembers the previous correction and may not need as much stimulation the next time.
- As your dog learns the purpose of the e-collar, he requires less stimulation—lower levels—for correction. However, if you take him hunting or to new training grounds, he may surprise you by not responding to stimulation. Move up to the next intensity level, matching the level of stimulation to your dog's level of excitement.
- Avoid saying "Whoa" and correcting your dog with the e-collar simultaneously. Use one or the other. If you tell your dog to "Whoa" at the same instant you touch him with stimulation, he learns to associate these two things. When you say "Whoa," he thinks he is going to receive stimulation. If he goes on point and you caution him by saying "Whoa," he gets nervous. Some dogs lose style, and others

leave point. The right way to do this is to caution him with "Whoa," and if he doesn't respond, then touch him with stimulation.

USING THE E-COLLAR FOR ATTENTION

Once your dog understands the purpose of the e-collar, you may use low levels of stimulation to get his attention. You can communicate with him by using the e-collar instead of using your voice or whistle.

In yard work, the dog learns that stimulation is a correction. Once he understands this lesson, the next step is to teach him to understand stimulation as a form of communication. If you touch your dog with a low level of stimulation, you notice that he looks up to see what you want. When your dog does this, you can begin to use stimulation to "talk" to him. If he is running down a tree line and you want him to turn to the right, you can either blow your whistle or touch him lightly with low stimulation. Both actions get his attention, and he looks up, sees you turning, and swings around with you.

Using low-level stimulation is like saying, "Hey, I want your attention." Most dogs like to please; they want to know what you want them to do, and they are happy to respond to you.

USING THE E-COLLAR FOR AVOIDANCE

You may use the e-collar at higher levels to teach your dog to avoid certain types of non-game species such as deer, turkeys, snakes, and so forth. To teach avoidance, use continuous stimulation.

To stop your dog from chasing deer, use a high level of continuous stimulation while he is chasing. Do not say anything. Your dog thinks that the deer is responsible for the unpleasant sensation and runs back to you for safety. He will be upset. If your dog is a hunting dog, you can reassure him. If he is a field trial dog, ignore him; otherwise, he may come back to you for reassurance every time he smells deer. Act as if you don't know what happened. It may take a couple of encounters with deer, but he will get the idea and learn to avoid them.

This technique can be used for breaking dogs off other types of trash (non-game species), but do not use it unless your dog shows an interest in chasing first.

AUTHORS' COMMENTARY

Your dog doesn't talk, so you have to set up situations using the e-collar to find out how much he knows. Watch his reactions; the dog tells you what he understands. If you introduce the e-collar properly, your dog will like it because it makes training easier for him to understand. He is able to figure out what you want him to do because he is corrected with the stimulation the instant he makes a mistake.

As your dog gets older, he should continue to wear the e-collar. You may not use it, but do keep it on him. If he makes a mistake, you can correct him and stay in control; consequently, he doesn't become collar-wise or develop bad habits. Remember that your dog should think of the e-collar as part of his uniform when he is afield. If you have done your job right, he will get excited when you put it on him.

THE MORE COMFORTABLE A DOG IS, THE FASTER HE LEARNS.

DAVE WALKER

CHAPTER SEVEN

Teaching Steady-to-Wing-and-Shot

A dog is steady-to-wing-and-shot when he points, remains staunch while the bird is flushed and fired at, and stands until the handler releases him. Another term that has the same meaning is *broke.* A dog is considered "broke" if he is steady-to-wing-and-shot. The steadying or breaking training is considered formal training, and is the process of redirecting your dog's desire to get birds for himself. This process goes against your dog's nature and his instinct to survive. Instead of hunting birds for himself, he is taught to hunt birds for you.

This chapter describes Dave Walker's method of teaching steady-to-wing-and-shot. Amateurs (both hunters and field trial competitors) have successfully trained their dogs using Dave's method. Dave teaches this process in two steps.

- Steady-to-wing: The dog holds point until the handler flushes, but he may break at the shot.
- Steady-to-shot: The dog stands through the shot until the handler releases him.

In this chapter Dave introduces the "whoa" and "here" commands and uses the e-collar at the same time that he is developing the dog's pointing instinct. While chapter 5 of this book discusses the fundamentals of yard work, and chapter 6 discusses training with the e-collar, this chapter tells you how to combine these commands and the e-collar with bird work. Some information from previous chapters is repeated here in order to fully explain Dave's training method.

The basic steps for teaching your dog to be steady-to-wing-and-shot should take about eight weeks. The section headings (given in weeks) are guidelines, not specific time tables, which are unrealistic in dog training because dogs learn at different rates. Do not be disappointed if your dog takes a little longer to catch on than the times given in these guidelines. The headings are just to give you a general idea of what to expect your dog to accomplish within a certain time frame.

The more excited your Brittany is around birds, the easier he is to break. Steadying him can temporarily diminish his desire to find birds, so don't begin unless he is fired-up. He needs to have had birds in his mouth, to have caught birds, and to have had birds shot for him before you begin this phase of his training. A general rule for a hunting dog is that he should have at least one hunting season under his belt. A field trial dog should finish his derby season before the formal breaking process begins, although initial steadying can start earlier. Your dog will let you know when he is ready to be broke by holding a point long enough for you to flush the bird.

Teaching Steady-to-Wing: DAVE WALKER

When Dave teaches a dog to be steady-to-wing, he works him every day. He begins by teaching the "whoa" and "here" commands with the check-cord, and at the same time he introduces the e-collar. The only time Dave talks to the dog is to give him verbal commands. Otherwise, he is silent. He tugs the check-cord or uses the e-collar to correct the dog; he strokes the dog to praise him; he taps the dog on the side to release him; he turns his body to indicate the direction he wants the dog to go. During each session, but separate from these lessons, Dave works the dog on birds to develop his pointing instinct. He doesn't fire a blank gun because gunfire increases a dog's level of excitement and makes it harder for him to control himself.

The First and Second Weeks

Before Dave begins the training session, he tethers two pigeons and plants them in the training field. Next, he gets the dog, puts the training collar behind the dog's identification collar and the e-collar in front of it. After snapping the check-cord to the training collar, he begins to teach the dog to walk on the loose check-cord. Once the dog is walking on the loose check-cord, Dave uses the check-cord to teach him to "stop and stand still" and to let Dave walk in front of him. When the dog stops and stands, Dave strokes him. At this time, he also introduces the "here" command by turning his body and walking in a different direction.

After a couple of repetitions of "stop and stand still" and "here," Dave works the dog on one of the pigeons that he has planted. He brings the dog into the bird downwind and across the scent because he wants the dog to get a nose full of scent. If he brings the dog in directly downwind of the bird, the dog may get a little scent and want to creep up closer to get more scent. Dave doesn't care if the dog points or makes a dive at the bird, just as long as he doesn't catch it before it flies. If the dog makes a dive at the bird and the bird doesn't fly, Dave restrains the dog with the check-cord so that he can kick the bird with his foot to get it to fly. (Because getting the bird in the air is so necessary to this type of training, it is important to have pigeons that are alert and are good fliers.) Dave keeps walking and lets the dog chase to the end of the check-cord. He is developing the dog's pointing instinct by letting him run at the bird and teaching him that he cannot catch it. (See chapter 3, Introducing Birds and Gunfire, Why Dogs Point.)

Bringing the Dog Downwind of the Scent:

The trainer brings the dog into the bird, downwind and across the scent.

As the dog chases the bird, Dave stops him by turning him in a slow circle before he hits the end of the check-cord because he doesn't want the dog to stop too suddenly. Once the dog has stopped, Dave strokes him for standing. He says, "Here" or taps the dog on the side to release him and walks in a direction different than the one in which the bird flew. He may also try to walk in front of the dog once he has stopped him, after the bird has flown.

Dave starts each session with a review of the commands and begins to introduce the e-collar to enforce them. In between the commands, he works the dog on birds. The dog becomes more excited as he chases the birds, so Dave begins to combine low stimulation with a tug of the check-cord to stop him when he gets to the end of the check-cord. Timing is critical, and for this reason, Dave uses a holster on his belt so that his hand rests on the transmitter with his fingers on the buttons. Dave tries to finish on a good note before he puts the dog up. The sessions last about fifteen minutes and get longer as the dog progresses in his training.

At the end of this training period, the dog has learned to "stop and stand still" when Dave tugs the check-cord, and he lets Dave walk in front of him. He turns and goes with Dave when Dave says, "Here," and he is becoming familiar with the e-collar. He points or doesn't point when he smells a bird and chases it to the end of the check-cord.

The Second and Third Weeks

During the second and third weeks of training, Dave continues to work the dog on the commands and uses the e-collar. As he reviews "stop and stand still," he drops the check-cord so he can get farther out in front of the dog for longer periods of time, and he pretends to flush a bird. Once the dog lets Dave kick around in front of him, Dave is ready to introduce "whoa" as a verbal command, speaking the word softly—one time. It usually only takes a couple of times before the dog is stopping when Dave says "Whoa."

Dave continues to work the dog on pigeons in between the commands. The dog may still dive at the bird before it flushes and chase it when it flies, but now Dave begins to stop him sooner. He waits until the bird is in the air and combines low stimulation with a tug of the check-cord to stop the dog in time to watch the bird fly off. Once the dog stops, Dave strokes him for standing. At this point Dave may try to walk in front of the dog and pretend to flush another bird.

The dog may begin to establish point during this period because Dave is taking the fun out of chasing. When the dog establishes point, Dave doesn't stop walking, but he holds the end of the check-cord and keeps walking toward the bird to flush it. If the dog breaks point as Dave walks in to flush, Dave waits until the bird flies before using stimulation with the check-cord. Dave does not want to use stimulation while the dog has scent of the bird and waits until the bird is in the air before he uses it.

At the end of this period, the dog has learned the "whoa"

command, and lets Dave walk out in front of him and pretend to flush. He may or may not begin to establish point. Dave stops him with stimulation and the check-cord in time to watch the bird fly off and practices walking in front of the dog once he is stopped.

The Third, Fourth, and Fifth Weeks

During the third, fourth, and fifth weeks, the dog should begin to establish point when he smells a pigeon. He may not hold for Dave to flush, but he should begin to point. The next step in the breaking process is using the e-collar by itself—not combining it with the tug of the check-cord—to discourage the dog from chasing the bird. Before the dog can advance to the next level, he must understand that stimulation is a correction for his behavior.

To determine how much the dog understands, Dave gives him a test: He drops the check-cord and lets the dog drag it, softly says "Whoa," and continues to walk—making the dog think that he is supposed to keep walking too. If the dog keeps walking, Dave touches him with low stimulation. If the dog stops, he understands the correction. If the dog becomes confused, Dave goes back a couple of steps and uses the check-cord to review the commands.

Once the dog understands that stimulation is a correction, Dave can use the e-collar—by itself—without a tug of the check-cord. Dave drops the check-cord and lets the dog drag it. The dog begins to hunt and establish point, but Dave knows that the dog may still dive at the bird when Dave walks in to flush it. If he dives at the bird, Dave stops him with just stimulation, once the bird is in the air. Dave strokes him for stopping, and together they watch the bird fly off.

At the end of this period, the dog understands the e-collar. He has begun to drag the check-cord, to establish point, and to hold until Dave gets there.

The Fourth, Fifth, and Sixth Weeks

During the fourth, fifth, and sixth weeks, Dave begins to use the e-collar when the dog is on point—when he is still breathing in the scent of the pigeon. For example, the dog goes on point and begins to creep when Dave walks in to flush. The moment that the dog lifts his front foot, Dave touches him with low stimulation. This correction can be used at this time because the dog understands that stimulation is a correction for not "stopping and standing still."

At this stage of training, Dave is using stimulation when the dog has scent of the bird. He uses the least amount of stimulation to get the job done, paying close attention to the dog to detect any signs that he doesn't understand the training. If Dave has to make a severe correction with the e-collar, or if the dog points with a low tail at any time during training, Dave shoots a bird for him and then puts him back in the kennel—thus ending the session on a positive note for the dog.

Teaching Steady-to-Shot:
DAVE WALKER

Once the dog points and is steady-to-wing, he is ready to be fired over. Knowing that gunfire excites the dog, Dave introduces gunfire by taking the dog back a couple of steps. Until now Dave has been letting the dog drag the check-cord, but this time when he goes in to flush, he holds the check-cord. He expects the dog to break at the shot, and he uses the check-cord—not the stimulation—to stop the dog if he chases. Dave also delays firing when he flushes the bird to help the dog understand that he is to remain standing. Once the dog understands that he is to stand when Dave fires, Dave uses the e-collar to correct him for moving. Usually, the dog learns to be steady-to-shot in two or three sessions.

The Seventh and Eighth Weeks

At this level in training, the dog establishes point and stands while Dave flushes and fires. He is almost steady-to-wing-and-shot in the training field, but Dave has to teach him to be more reliable. Dogs, like people, learn from their mistakes, and this is an important step in the training process.

Now Dave is ready to teach the dog that he should always hold point. If the dog is on point with birds in front of him, he must learn to stand there no matter what happens. Dave can tap him on his side, call to him, or blow his whistle. It doesn't matter what Dave does—the dog should remain on point. To teach this lesson, Dave has to wait for an opportunity. (This is a situation in which the dog points, moves up, and points again.) When the dog does this, Dave encourages him to move up again and take out the bird (flush a bird he should point). He taps the dog on his side or blows his whistle. If the dog dives for the bird, Dave corrects him with the e-collar. Dave is teaching the dog that he has to stand there when birds are in front of him.

Now is also the time to work on relocations. Again, Dave waits for an opportunity. If the dog goes on point and Dave can see the bird, he pretends to flush but he is careful not to disturb the bird. The dog thinks that Dave can't find it. Dave walks back to the dog and taps him on the side. If the dog doesn't move, Dave flushes the bird, fires, and pets the dog. If the dog dives for the bird, Dave uses the e-collar to correct him.

The Eighth Week

At this point in training the dog is *green broke* (recently broke). He has learned to be steady-to-wing-and-shot in the training field while dragging the check-cord and working on pigeons, but this is all that he knows. Anytime Dave introduces something new to him, he has to be retaught. He has to learn to listen to Dave when he is not dragging the check-cord. He has to learn to be steady on quail and other game birds and to obey commands at new training and hunting grounds. The hard work has just begun.

If he is a hunting dog, he wears the e-collar whenever he is afield. Dave keeps him under control and doesn't let him range out of sight. If he takes out birds, Dave can see him and correct him. If he is a field trial dog, he always wears the e-collar in training. Since he is not allowed to wear an e-collar in competition, he may be one or two seasons away from being reliable on his birds at a trial.

Shooting Birds

There are times in steady-to-wing-and-shot training when it is desirable to shoot a bird for the dog. Before beginning steady-to-wing training, Dave may shoot a bird so the dog can get it in his mouth and taste it. In this situation Dave walks the dog on a check-cord to a planted bird. He keeps walking—letting the dog point, pounce, or do whatever he wants to do—and flushes the bird. Once the bird is in the air, Dave fires. Sometimes he holds the check-cord and walks with the dog to the downed bird. Other times he drops the check-cord and lets the dog run to the bird.

During the steadying process, Dave may have to make a severe correction or the dog may signal that he is losing interest in birds by pointing with a lower tail. In these situations, Dave shoots a bird for him. At this level in training, Dave doesn't let him retrieve the bird. He makes the dog remain standing while he gets the bird and throws it back to him to mouth. Generally, the taste of the bird rekindles the dog's desire to find birds.

If Dave wants to shoot a bird for the dog that is steady-to-shot and have him retrieve it, Dave makes the dog stand after the shot until he releases him by tapping him on the side. The dog then retrieves the bird.

AUTHORS' COMMENTARY

Some things make sense to people but they don't make sense to dogs. Other things make sense to dogs, but they don't make sense to people. Dave's method may not make sense to you, especially the no-talking part, but it will make sense to your dog. Your dog prefers an e-collar correction to being yelled at. He knows you are pleased with him when you pet him, and he wants to go with you because you are his friend.

Each dog is different, and this is where good breeding pays off. The more natural pointing instinct and trainability your dog has, the faster he progresses in training. For this reason it is important to have field trial stock in your dog's pedigree. Field trial dogs have proven their ability to perform at the highest levels of competition.

If you want to teach your dog to be steady-to-wing, or wing-and-shot, you will find few activities as rewarding as teaching him. You may not get the polish or reliability a professional does, and you will probably have a few headaches along the way, but you will develop a sense of pride in your training ability, and you will create a bond between you and your dog that is special and rewarding.

> KEEP TRAINING BLACK AND WHITE FOR THE DOG.
>
> MAURICE LINDLEY

CHAPTER EIGHT

Providing Additional Training

Stop-to-flush, backing, and retrieving are discussed here because you introduce them after your Brittany has learned the basic commands and behaviors. Stop-to-flush training can begin around the time that you are teaching him to be steady-to-wing. Once your dog understands stop-to-flush, you can teach him backing. You may also introduce retrieving at this time. The retrieving section includes a special technique for puppies that reinforces their basic retrieving instinct.

TEACHING STOP-TO-FLUSH

The purpose of *stop-to-flush* training is to teach your dog to "stop and stand still" when he sees a bird flush that he can't see or smell. Whether you hunt or field trial, your dog should understand that birds in the air mean "stop and stand still" until released. Stop-to-flush situations can occur anytime you and your dog are afield—birds can get up on their own, be accidentally flushed by your dog when he is upwind of them, or you can accidentally flush them.

There are three important reasons to teach stop-to-flush:

- In covey situations when some birds fly and other birds hold, your dog won't flush any birds that still remain on the ground.

- Hunting dogs that are steady-to-wing but not steady-to-shot are less likely to bump and chase birds and more willing to hold point and wait for you to flush.
- Field trial dogs are expected to stop-to-flush.

Stop-to-Flush:
MAURICE LINDLEY

Most dogs want to chase when they see birds flush. Maurice uses bird launchers to teach the dog that birds in the air mean "stop and stand still." He launches birds in front of the dog that the dog can't see or smell, and restrains the dog from chasing with the check-cord and eventually the e-collar. Maurice prefers remote launchers for stop-to-flush work, so he can flush birds at a distance from the dog. Manual launchers also work if you attach strings to the release levers and lay them on the ground where you plan to launch the birds.

To begin, Maurice puts pigeons in two or three launchers and plants the launchers in light cover around the training field. To remember the exact location of the launchers, Maurice puts them next to cover that looks different. He gets the dog, puts on the training collar and e-collar, and walks the dog on the check-cord upwind to the first launcher. As the dog is about 50 feet away and moving in the direction of the launcher, Maurice releases the pigeon. If the dog chases, Maurice stops him with the check-cord. Maurice never says "Whoa." He repeats this sequence on the second and third launcher.

During the next few weeks, Maurice works the dog on stop-to-flush a couple of times a week. If the dog continues to run at the birds when they flush, Maurice stops him with the check-cord and reviews stop and stand still. He may begin to spin the dog. Once the dog understands that he is not supposed to chase, Maurice uses the e-collar to stop him from chasing, but he is careful to keep the dog away from the launcher. If the dog gets too close to the launcher, Maurice does not use the e-collar because the dog may smell or see the launcher and associate it with the stimulation. Once Maurice can stop the dog from chasing with the stimulation, he drops the check-cord and lets the dog drag it, so the dog is moving freely before the bird is released.

The next step is planting two launchers together. Maurice drops the check-cord as the dog is moving and releases the first bird. The dog stops. He walks in front of the dog, and, as he is walking, releases the second bird. If the dog stands still, he fires the blank gun because he is in front of the dog. Using multiple birds at this stage in training helps the dog understand the reason to stop-to-flush.

TEACHING BACKING

Backing occurs when a dog stops and stands at the sight of another dog on rigid point. A dog that demonstrates a willingness to back, and does so with style, is a pleasure to behold. Some dogs have more backing instinct than others, but for a dog to be reliable, he needs to be taught to back.

Many professionals have numerous broke dogs that they use to teach backing. The single dog owner may use a silhouette—a wood or metal cutout of a dog on point—to teach backing. You can buy one (see appendix A), or you can make one from 3/8-inch plywood, cutting the board into the shape of a Brittany on point. Paint both sides realistically and attach one or two metal stakes at the base of the form that, when driven into the ground, hold the silhouette upright.

Backing:
JIM BASHAM

Jim Basham uses the silhouette to teach backing as a stop-to-flush command. In order to use this method, the dog must first understand stop-to-flush. To begin, Jim uses a remote launcher with a quail or pigeon and a silhouette. A manual launcher also works if you attach a string to the release lever and lay the string on the ground where you plan to stop the dog. Jim positions the silhouette behind a bush or at the end of a mowed strip—someplace that the dog can't see it until he is very close. He puts the launcher near the silhouette, and, if the dog can see it, covers the launcher with a light layer of leaves or grass.

Jim puts the check-cord and e-collar on the dog and walks him around. He doesn't walk the dog directly to the silhouette but lets him hunt at the end of the check-cord. Next, he walks the dog toward the silhouette, being careful to bring him in on the upwind side because he doesn't want the dog to smell the bird. If he smells the bird, he is not backing. When the dog sees the silhouette, it surprises him, and he hesitates. Jim lets him stand there for a few seconds before releasing the bird. Jim does not say "Whoa." He releases the bird and does not fire a blank gun. He lets the dog stand there and mark the bird. Jim turns and walks the dog back the way he came, being careful not to walk him past the silhouette.

Jim continues to work the dog every day but changes the location of the setup and keeps the sessions short. When the dog sees the silhouette, he begins to anticipate the bird flying and starts to stop on his own. Jim's goal is to get out in front of the dog. At first, when the dog stops, Jim holds the check-cord as he walks in front of the dog. Eventually, Jim is able to drop the check-cord. The dog begins to stand while Jim walks past the silhouette and kicks his feet in a mock flushing attempt. Jim may even stroke the silhouette before he releases the bird. He begins to fire the blank gun once he can get in front of the dog. Jim varies the number of launchers, flying one bird and then another. Sometimes he carries birds in his pocket and throws them as he flushes behind the silhouette. Jim still hasn't said "Whoa."

Backing a Silhouette:

When the dog sees the silhouette, he begins to anticipate a bird flying and begins to stop on his own.

Jim begins to use the e-collar once the dog understands that he must stop when he sees the silhouette. If Jim is in front of him, and he picks up a foot, Jim can touch him with low stimulation. But if Jim needs to use a higher level of stimulation to stop him, Jim goes back and reviews stop-to-flush before using the e-collar again, because the dog hasn't learned to stop when he sees the silhouette.

Once Jim teaches the dog to honor the silhouette, he has to teach him to back a live dog. (Ask a buddy with a broke dog to help you.) The steps are similar, except that the live dog may make the backing dog more competitive, so the backing dog may be less willing to honor him. Jim has an assistant handle the broke dog and work him on a bird so that he establishes point. Next, Jim brings in the other dog on a check-cord. As he did with the silhouette, he brings the dog in so that he doesn't see the pointing dog until he is close, and he makes sure that he can't smell the bird. This takes careful planning. Jim gives the backing dog a chance to back on his own. If he doesn't stop, Jim carefully picks him up, sets him back, and says "Whoa." Once he stops, Jim stands next to him with a loose check-cord as the assistant flushes the bird and fires in front of the pointing dog. Jim lets the dog mark the bird. The reward for backing is getting to see the bird fly. Jim walks him away from the area and pets him for a job well done.

As Jim progresses, he changes the angle of approach. He brings the backing dog into the pointing dog from the front and from the side. Occasionally, he allows the backing dog to come in from behind where he can smell the bird. He also works in different locations. Jim says the key to teaching a dog to back is not saying "Whoa" too soon. The dog must learn to make the decision to stop on his own.

TEACHING RETRIEVING

Professionals that specialize in training Brittanys do not like to teach force retrieving. The *force-retrieve* uses force, such as pinching a toe or an ear, to train a dog to retrieve. If a dog must be a reliable retriever to compete in events that require retrieving, then he should be force-trained; however, force retrieving is not discussed in this book. There are some excellent books to help you with this method (see Bibliography), as well as trainers that specialize in this type of instruction.

Fortunately, many Brittanys have strong retrieving instincts that can be developed without force. Dave Walker has developed some techniques to effectively teach dogs to retrieve by encouraging them to retrieve as puppies. Sometimes this training is enough for them to become reliable retrievers. Bill Gibbons has other techniques for encouraging dogs that like to carry objects around in their mouths but don't want to pick up birds to retrieve.

Retrieving for Pups:
DAVE WALKER

Dave likes to teach a puppy to hold a small paint roller (3 inches long by 1 inch wide) when he is nine to ten weeks old. The pup has to be physically big enough to hold the roller in his mouth. Dave stands the pup on a table and attaches the check-cord to the pup's collar. Dave gently opens the pup's mouth and slides in the roller. He gives a gentle tug with the check-cord and says "Hold." His left hand carefully holds the pup's mouth closed so that he doesn't drop it. Dave strokes the pup a couple of times, says "Give," and then takes the roller. If the pup doesn't want to release it, Dave gently pushes the roller back into the pup's mouth, causing him to release it. Dave praises the pup and puts him on the ground. Dave never has the pup hold the roller for too long. In the beginning, he wants the pup to take the roller in his mouth and hold it for a short period of time. As the training progresses, Dave increases the length of time that the pup holds the roller in his mouth. After about a week, the pup stands still and holds the roller while Dave strokes him.

Next, Dave tosses a small metal can (such as a tomato paste can) that is covered with two or three quail wings secured by thin wire. The pup doesn't mouth the can (play with it in his mouth) because the surface is hard, but the taste of the wings excites him. Dave says "Fetch," and the pup—still wearing the check-cord—runs to get the can. If he doesn't want to bring it back, Dave encourages him to bring it with gentle tugs on the check-cord. He praises him and then throws the can again. For many dogs, this type of retrieving is enough to make them reasonably good retrievers.

Retrieving for the Adult Dog:
BILL GIBBONS

Some dogs enjoy retrieving all kinds of objects, but they won't pick up birds. When Bill gets a dog in for training that doesn't like to retrieve birds, he begins working with him on retrieving as the breaking process progresses. Every once in a while, as the dog is being steadied, Bill shoots a bird for him. If the dog doesn't want to retrieve it, Bill walks the dog on the check-cord to the downed bird. When the dog reaches down to smell the bird, Bill praises him. He pets him and says "Good boy," to let him know that he has done a good job. He praises the dog for acknowledging the bird.

The next time Bill shoots a bird the dog may try to pick it up. If he doesn't pick it up, Bill continues to praise him. If he does pick it up, Bill is careful not to pull or call the dog to him. If the dog acts like he wants to hold the bird in his mouth, Bill walks with him. Again, he never asks the dog to bring the bird to him. If the dog carries the bird a little way and drops it, Bill praises him again. Often the dog hears the excitement in Bill's voice and picks up the bird again.

As the dog nears the end of his training, he is steady on his game. He is pointing and letting Bill flush. Up to now Bill has praised the dog for any interest he has shown in picking up and carrying the bird. At this point, Bill stops shooting birds for the dog. The dog has been taught the "here" command, but, at this point, Bill is going to use the "here" command to mean "come to me immediately." He stops using "here" to tell the dog to "go with me."

Once the dog is responding immediately to the "here" command, Bill is ready to introduce retrieving. He lets the dog run and point a bird. He walks in, flushes it, and kills it. When the bird falls, he releases the dog. The dog goes out and picks up the bird. Bill commands "Here," and nine times out of ten the dog is obedient and runs to Bill. He is not thinking about dropping the bird; he is thinking about obeying the command. Bill does this only one time. He doesn't want to overdo it. Eventually this dog becomes a good retriever.

AUTHORS' COMMENTARY

The extent of training that your dog receives is up to you. A dog that stops-to-flush demonstrates good manners by not chasing birds in the air or flushing other birds that may still remain on the ground. Backing also shows good manners; no one likes to run with a dog that steals another dog's point. A dog that delivers a bird-to-hand is more impressive than a dog that points a dead bird, but, in either case, the game is rarely lost. If you are a hunter, you may want your dog steady-to-wing, stopping-to-flush, breaking at shot, and retrieving-to-hand.

If you compete in American Field and/or AKC field trials, your dog should be steady-to-wing-and-shot. He should stop-to-flush, and back a bracemate that is on rigid point. Whatever you may choose to teach your dog, remember—the only person he has to please is you.

DOG TRAINING IS LEARNING HOW TO COMMUNICATE.

TOMMY TRACY

CHAPTER NINE

Talking with Professionals

Professionals use different methods to train their dogs, and they end up with similar results. Successful professionals understand that the thinking behind the training is as important as the specific training steps. They realize that the dogs have to understand what the trainers are asking them to do, and that training methods are not chiseled in stone.

The first section in this chapter contains paraphrased conversations with three professionals—Ben Lorenson, Gene Stewart, and Tommy Tracy. They discuss common training problems that you may encounter as you train your Brittany. The second section is a paraphrased conversation with Maurice Lindley about how he starts the young dog to prepare him for formal training.

SOLVING PROBLEMS

Aggression

How do you stop a dog from being aggressive?

Ben Lorenson: The dog may be aggressive because he wants to dominate the other dog. You can fix this type of aggression with the e-collar, but you need to fix it right away. Don't let it escalate. If, on the other hand, the dog becomes aggressive because he's afraid, then the e-collar can make it worse.

Some young dogs want to try out being aggressive to dominate the other dog. About the time that you're breaking him is about the time that the aggression starts. His confidence is high, and he thinks he's king of the world. Just when he thinks he's tough, I show him I'm tougher. Some of them come out of it, but some get worse. It's like two teenagers wrestling; but if one of them wants to kill the other, you can't let him play anymore.

Gene Stewart: This problem is always a tough one. I'd use the e-collar. If he's a field trial dog, you should set up a situation similar to a trial. You break your dog away, and I break my dog away. As soon as my dog goes over to your dog, I'd be getting on him with the e-collar. You can stop aggressive behavior in your dog, but he may throw it in his pups.

Tommy Tracy: The problem lies in the fact that when one dog's going after the other dog, most people stop. They just stop. Don't stop; keep going—keep walking or keep riding. Don't go in the same direction as your dog. Go the other way and call him. Yell "Hey!" If he doesn't turn, yell "Hey" again, and touch him with the e-collar. You want him to think the stimulation is a correction for not coming with you.

Go somewhere else. The dog's still thinking about fighting, or, maybe now, he's actually nervous. Get him away. Get him by himself.

Blinking

What do you do to stop a dog from blinking (avoiding game)?

Ben Lorenson: First you have to figure out why the dog blinks. Nine times out of ten, it's the result of misusing the "whoa" command. For example, the dog's on point and starts to creep. You say "Whoa" and touch him with the e-collar at the same time. The dog leaves because he thinks that every time you say "Whoa," he gets hit with the e-collar. He's not blinking the bird; he's blinking the word "whoa." The dog has to understand that he's not going to be hit with the e-collar when you say "Whoa." He has to think that because he didn't "whoa," he's going to get hit with the e-collar. That's a big difference. Use one or the other, but don't say "Whoa" and use the e-collar simultaneously.

Gene Stewart: I'd quit training him. I'd take him to the field and shoot some birds, maybe every other day for a week. I'd walk in, flush the bird, and kill it. If he didn't want to get the bird, I'd get it for him. I'd let him munch on it a little and maybe take the head off and give it to him to see if he'd eat it.

Tommy Tracy: Blinkers think they're going to get in trouble when the bird gets up. The bird makes them nervous, so they're avoiding the situation. I'd go back in training. I'd "whoa" him. Then I'd throw birds for him. I might even give him a bird to eat. He might begin to think, "Hey, this isn't so bad."

Deer Chasing

How do you stop a dog from chasing deer?

Ben Lorenson: A dog's natural instinct is to find game. If he's not finding birds, he'll find something else—deer, rabbits, whatever.

A hunting dog gets into deer because the hunter walks down the deer trail. It's the path of least resistance. The dog also runs down the deer trail because it's the path of least resistance, and of course, the same is true for the deer. When the hunter, the dog, and the deer all use the same trail, the dog will find the deer.

If the dog's been on enough birds first, the problem is easy to fix with the e-collar. The dog learns that not every scent is something to be chased. But I don't like to get a dog off deer until he's confident around his game—until he's looking for birds. I don't want to ruin his desire to hunt.

Gene Stewart: The biggest problem with stopping field trial dogs from chasing deer is the fact that they don't get into enough deer at an early age. It's easier to break them off deer when they're young, but make sure that they know how to hunt for birds first. I use an e-collar, but the amount of stimulation I use depends on the dog. Some dogs take a lot; others don't need as much.

Tommy Tracy: Get dogs into deer early. When they are puppies, I take them out to find deer. If you can get them into deer when they are young, you're better off. Dogs chase deer because they're bored. They're not finding enough birds.

Their initial reaction to a deer when it gets up is, "Whoa, what is this?" The big scent and the flash of the white tail excite them. It's easy to fix the problem with a young dog. You touch him with the e-collar in a couple of instances like this and go on. But you touch him only if he shows an interest. And be sure to start out slowly.

It's harder to fix this problem with an older dog. He already has the desire to chase, and now you're burning him with the e-collar. As a result of the severe corrections, he doesn't want to run anymore because he's bumping into deer scent everywhere he goes.

Flagging

How do you stop a dog from flagging (moving his tail while on point)?

Ben Lorenson:: Some dogs flag because scenting conditions aren't right, like in the spring when the birds are molting or in the summer when the birds are hatching young and put off little scent. It's unnatural to work dogs during these times.

Fifty percent of dogs flag during the breaking process. Some of them flag because they want to knock the bird, and some flag from a lack of confidence. When you break a dog, you take away his confidence. If you finish breaking him, the problem usually clears up. Most come out of it, but some don't.

Gene Stewart: You can fix the problem, but sooner or later it'll come back. I think flagging is genetic. If the tail's up in the air and flagging, it's genetic. But if it's down and flagging, it's from pressure—pressure caused by too much voice or too much *whoa*-ing. Sometimes flagging is the result of picking up the dog and setting him back. I use the e-collar to stop a dog from moving on his birds, and once I stop him, I don't set him back. I just leave him there to think about it. I do not walk over to him and put my hands on him.

You might cure some dogs by shooting birds for them. I've also tried using the e-collar on the belly. Some dogs will stop flagging, but then they'll start again in a couple of days.

Tommy Tracy: Flagging is a tough problem because there are so many causes for it. There's the genetics part. There's the people part. There's the dog's part—flagging because he wants to bump the bird. To fix the problem, you have to identify it.

If the handler has caused the problem, he should be quiet. Don't say "Whoa." In fact, don't say anything. Let the dog work it out by himself. People think they're helping him by whoa-ing him before the bird. Let him take it out if he wants to.

Gun-Shyness

How do you cure a gun-shy dog?

Ben Lorenson: I see more hunting dogs with this problem than I do field trial dogs. There are two reasons for hunting dogs being gun-shy. First, as young puppies in the house, they were corrected with a rolled-up newspaper, so they have a negative association with loud noise. Second, in the field they won't leave you far enough so that you can shoot the gun without it blasting their ears. You need to fix gun-shyness at the first sign. Too many dogs I get in are already leaving when I pull out the gun. You need to go back and introduce gunfire again, as you did when he was a puppy. Gunfire should be a reward for a dog. The shot means that the birds are flying. The dog needs to think of it as a reward.

Gene Stewart: As far as fixing the problem, I'd go to the barrel. I'd throw birds for him the first week. If he comes off the barrel, set him back up. You want to make him bold. Then the second week, I'd throw some birds and shoot the gun. He has to stand on that barrel. If he's afraid and jumps off, pick him up and put him back on the barrel. You're almost force-breaking him to the gun.

Tommy Tracy: First, don't create the problem. Don't assume he's not going to be gun-shy. Introduce gunfire in a nice, easy way.

Now, for a dog that's already gun-shy, I'd reintroduce the gun as if he were a puppy. I'd go backward. When I go to feed him, I'd fire. When he's out running, I'd fire.

Sitting or Lying Down on Point

How do you stop a dog from sitting or lying down on point?

Ben Lorenson: Some dogs sit because they're house dogs, and they were taught to sit. If this is the reason for the problem, you can put the e-collar on his belly to teach him not to sit.

Some dogs sit because they are under too much pressure. The dog may have enough pointing instinct so that he doesn't want to leave the bird, but he's confused and doesn't know what to do, so he sits. Sometimes using the e-collar on the belly creates more pressure. If this is the case, it may be better to ignore the behavior and let it work itself out.

Gene Stewart: Why is he sitting down in the first place? He may be sitting or lying down because you're yanking on his neck. If you keep yanking him back and pulling on him, pretty soon he's just going to relax and sit down. If you start with the e-collar on his belly, you won't have this problem.

Tommy Tracy: Put the e-collar on his belly when you start on birds, and you'll eliminate the problem. When you work a dog on birds, always have the e-collar on the belly.

Trailing

What do you do about a puppy that trails another dog?

Ben Lorenson:I There are a couple of reasons dogs trail other dogs. We breed a field trial dog to be competitive. We're actually breeding him to compete with the other dog. If one dog is more physically or mentally advanced than the other, the other dog will always be behind. Another reason for trailing is that the dog lacks confidence, and he lets the other dog lead him around.

The way to fix trailing is to teach the dog to hunt for himself. He has to learn what he's being competitive for *before* he competes. He's not in a race; he's competing to find birds.

Gene Stewart: I'd put out a bunch of birds on a tree line, and I'd cut loose the trailing pup with another pup. He'll probably chase the other pup around for a while. The other pup is going to find a bird first, and they'll both chase it, but, eventually, he'll find his own bird to chase and he'll forget about the other dog.

Tommy Tracy: My first reaction to this problem is that he's going to learn to hunt and find birds by himself. When you work him on birds, you're changing his objective about what he wants to do.

DEVELOPING THE YOUNG DOG

Describe how you start the young dog to prepare him for formal training.

Maurice Lindley: If I have a litter of pups, I like to start walking them as a group in the field at seven or eight weeks old. I want them to get used to the area before introducing them to birds. When they are three months old, I start exposing them to quail. I plant a couple of birds where they are easy to find.

I don't try to teach little puppies anything; I want to imprint birds and hunting early on and get them excited. I plant a couple of birds where they are easy to find. If they point, that's great. If they find birds and chase them, or if they find them and watch them fly off, that's fine. I want a puppy to come along at his own pace. A lot of people make mistakes working their puppies on too many birds. What works best is to have only one or two birds out.

If a puppy points a bird, I don't run up and flush it. I just stand back and observe. I stand there and let the puppy stand there on point. Then, all of a sudden, the puppy may want to get a little closer. Maybe the bird's running a bit, and I'll see the puppy start trying to figure out things. Maybe he sees something move, and he jumps in, and the bird gets up, and the puppy chases. I use good flying birds, so the puppy can't catch the bird, but if it happens, it's really not a big deal—more of a non-event. I pet the puppy, take the bird away, and go on.

I want to see puppies that get excited when I turn them loose and puppies that go out and look for birds. At first, I may have to walk them around and help them find birds before they find birds. I'll go with the puppies and I won't do a lot of change of direction, so they learn I'm going to stay in contact with them. This builds confidence. After two or three times exposing them to birds, a puppy should be thinking about birds. He's thinking, *Oh, I'm out here again, and I'm going to find birds!* That's where the hunting part starts. When they start doing that, I quit helping them. I just stand around and let them find birds on their own. Now it's really important not to overdo bird exposure. By four months old, they get bird exposure once a week. They might get walked in the field three days a week, but I put out birds one day a week. I don't want finding birds to seem too easy.

If I have just one puppy, that's okay too; I'll work him the same way I would a group of puppies. Say I get a puppy to start for a customer: I won't put birds out for a time or two. I'll get the puppy used to the new environment before I put out a couple of birds.

I use the best flying birds I can find because that's what puts point in the puppy. That's what develops the puppy in a natural way. He learns that when he smells the bird, he better stand there and point. When he moves a little closer—*boom*, that bird is up and gone. He learns to respect the bird. When the puppy is little, he's not strong enough to run a good flying bird down and catch it, so I like to expose him to birds early on before he gets some legs under him. I don't want him to learn he can catch a bunch of birds.

Around five months old, I start snapping the check-cord to the puppy's ID collar. I'm going to let him drag the check-cord to get him used to it because the check-cord is a big part of what I'll use to train him. Every time I take him out of the kennel, I put on the check-cord and lead him to the field. I stop him real easy—I don't fight with him—and I'll get him to be still for a second or two. Then I'll tap him to release him. That's the beginning stage of teaching a dog to stop and stand still. I can teach a puppy so much just by exposure. Before long that puppy learns he has to stop and stand still before I release him. When a puppy gets real bold hunting and chasing birds, I'm going to introduce the gun.

Around eight to nine months old, the puppy is physically strong enough to chase a quail down, so I quit working him on pen-raised quail. I don't want him making a ton of mistakes that I have to overcome when I start breaking him. I'm not worried about losing any "bird dog"—I've already imprinted that. I may still expose him to birds, but only if I have full-grown, flight-conditioned chukar, Hungarian partridge, or wild birds. He needs time to mature, until he is physically and mentally ready to start formal training at around one and a half years old.

This is a good time to take a puppy hunting. Hunting makes a bird dog, and I haven't started to break him yet. He doesn't have to be perfect. If he'll let me get close before helping me flush, I'm going to try to shoot the bird for him, but I'm not going to shoot bumped birds or birds he runs over. I want to show him the big picture—he points the bird, and boss man comes up there and gets him the bird. Getting the bird in his mouth shows him there's more to it than pointing and watching birds fly off. If I go to a shooting preserve, I'll try to hunt a puppy on chukar or Hungarian partridge. Ten good bird contacts are plenty for half a day. I don't need to kill a lot of birds, but the first season can be very productive hunting for a puppy.

> **MAN INTEGRATES THE DOG'S HUNTING INTO HIS OWN AND SO RAISES HUNTING TO ITS MOST COMPLEX AND PERFECT FORM**
>
> **JOSE ORTEGA Y GASSET**

CHAPTER TEN

Reflecting

Dogs' hunting instincts are superior to that of human beings. Dogs hunted on their own long before people asked them to hunt for them. In return for finding game, they were given food, shelter, and affection. The bond between dogs and people dates back to the Paleolithic Age, and while it's something that is easily felt, it's not easily described. This book contains some of the best professional training techniques for an amateur, but you can learn only so much from books. To understand these techniques, you have to do more than just read about them; you have to train with your dog. Just as he needs to learn the lessons that you are teaching him, you need to learn the lessons that he is teaching you. Only in this way can you realize the full joy of hunting with your dog and being part of a real team.

The following two anecdotes reflect the authors' appreciation and love of dogs.

Japanese Tea Bowls and Bird Dogs

Shoji Hamada was a gifted Japanese potter who was named a living National Treasure in 1955. Most of Hamada's life was dedicated to creating simple utilitarian objects, such as tea bowls that were unassuming and beautiful. He believed that the objects he created were born, not made. By reacting to the material rather than imposing his will on the form, his pieces had a natural appearance, a closeness to nature that looked neither mechanical nor man-made. He once explained that it had taken him thirty years to learn how to make pottery, thirty years to unlearn, and now he was ready to begin learning.

A pro trainer I know describes training a bird dog in a similar fashion, only he uses the face of a clock. He says people begin their training at the top, at twelve o'clock. As they learn, they descend. They think they are getting better, but, actually, they are getting worse. About the time they think they know everything, they are at six o'clock. Once they realize that dog training isn't as simple as they thought it was, and that maybe they don't know everything, they begin to ascend, eventually returning to twelve o'clock, where they began. This analogy may explain why a person's first dog is often the best dog and why it is so hard to have a great second dog. The problem doesn't lie so much with the dogs as with the trainers, their expectations, and the fact that they take credit for their first dog's success.

How well I know this scenario. My first field trial dog was a big winning dog. A couple of dogs followed, each a little more broken in spirit, until I found myself with a one-year-old pup I had corrected for just about everything her predecessors had done wrong. I started to turn upwards on the face of the clock when I realized that each dog is an individual, and that sound bird dog training has to be a reaction to an individual dog's actions. It is not imposing my will to create something mechanical or man-made. I had to learn to think like a beginner again. I had to unlearn everything.

As I unlearn, I begin to see that each dog is unique. I begin to understand when to build independence and when to take some of it away. I understand the difference between dogs that are tough in the kennel and dogs that are tough around their game. I learn to let the dog tell me when he is ready to be "broke" rather than breaking him the summer of his second year. I learn to correct a dog on deer only if he chases them.

Most importantly, I learn how much uncertainty there is in bird dog training. The more I learn, the less I know. In the words of the pro trainer: "It's a guess. You never really know." But it takes someone who has learned to train bird dogs and then unlearned it . . . who has gone from twelve o'clock to six o'clock and then back to twelve o'clock again to admit this. Maybe like the potter, the job of the trainer is not to impose his will but to be humble and unassuming, so that the beauty of the bird dog shines through. Perhaps, like the Japanese tea bowl, a bird dog is born—not made.

Martha H. Greenlee

(FIRST APPEARED IN *FIELD TRIAL MAGAZINE*, SPRING ISSUE, 2003, REPRINTED WITH PERMISSION)

The Eyes Have It

As I gently move the balls of my thumbs over his cheeks, the dog's eyes close. A moment later, they open. So much trust. I cradle his head in the palm of my hands, rubbing behind his ears with my forefingers as I continue to speak in a quiet voice. His sparkling eyes are open, a portal into the very depth of his essence. Their centers, the irises, are almost pitch black, surrounded by a rim of golden brown. I ponder what this Brittany is thinking, and wonder if he thinks at all. Does he have a soul? Maybe someday I will find the answer.

What I do know is that he can't seem to get close enough to me. He wraps one leg around my forearm and rolls his head to one side and looks into my face. He stares with fixed, wide-open eyes, then turns away quickly. In just a moment he looks back again with that calm, trusting, intent expression.

In a way I am transfixed, held motionless by the pup's gaze. I dream, forming a mental image of this pup casting along a fencerow, whirling ninety degrees, freezing on his first quail point, holding for a moment, and then pouncing to flush the bird. He chases, trying to catch the quail, but to no avail. Twenty or thirty yards into the pursuit, the Brit turns and comes back to me. His eyes ask: *Did I do good, Boss?* He sure did.

A moist tongue licks my chin and brings me out of my trance. The dog's gaze is again fixed on mine. The eyes have it.

David A. Webb

(FIRST APPEARED IN *FEISTY LITTLE POINTING DOG*, SILVER QUILL PRESS, CAMDEN, MAINE, 2000, REPRINTED WITH PERMISSION)

APPENDIX A

Resources

Bird Dog and Tack Supplies

GUN DOG SUPPLY
(800) 624-6378
www.gundogsupply.com

LION COUNTRY SUPPLY
(800) 662–5202
www.lcsupply.com

ROCK STEADY KENNEL AND SUPPLIES
(570) 638–2311
rocksteadykennel@hotmail.com
www.rocksteadykennelandsupplies.com

TARPIN HILL SADDLE COMPANY
(800) 354–8964
www.tarpinhill.com

TRAIL BLAZIN' INNOVATIONS (TBI)
(281) 530–3916
www.tbicatalog.com

Bird Supplies

FOY'S PIGEON SUPPLIES
(877) 355–7727
www.foyspigeonsupplies.com

G.Q.F. MANUFACTURING COMPANY
(912) 236–0651
www.gqfmfg.com

QUALITY WILDLIFE SERVICES, INC.
(877) 242–2482
info@qualitywildlife.com
www.qualitywildlife.com

Brittany Breeders and Events

AMERICAN BRITTANY CLUB
P.O. Box 1945
Pelham, AL 35124-5945
(205) 790–2133
http://clubs.akc.org/brit/

AMERICAN FIELD
542 South Dearborn St.,
Chicago, IL 60605
(312) 663–9797
www.americanfield.com

AMERICAN KENNEL CLUB
(919) 233–9767
www.akc.org

E-Collars

COLLAR CLINIC
1517 Northern Star Drive
Traverse City, MI 49686
(800) 430-2010
www.collarclinic.com

DOGTRA
1250 E. 223rd Street
Suite 119
Carson, CA 90745
(888) 811-9111
info@dogtra.com
www.dogtra.com

D.T. SYSTEMS, INC.
2872 Walnut Hill Lane
Dallas, TX 75229
(888) 588-8364
www.dtsystems.com

INNOTEK
1000 Fuller Drive
Garrett, IN 46738
(800) 826-5527
www.innotek.com

TRI-TRONICS
P.O. Box 17660
Tucson, AZ 85731
(800) 456-4343
www.tritronics.com

Training Collars and Videotapes

DAVE AND FAY WALKER
The Walker Plantation
(208) 278-5074
www.davewalkerdogs.com

HIGGINS GUNDOGS
P.O. Box 249
Roseville, CA 95678
(916) 717-5597
www.higginsgundogs.com

APPENDIX B

Recalling Quail

Quail instinctively flock together. A flock of quail is called a *covey*. If a covey is separated, the birds find each other by calling. When you release quail for training, you can recall them to a specific training area or to a quail house or recall pen by using a bird that you have confined in a certain place. This bird is called a *call bird* because it will call other birds to join it. If you have a quail feeder near the call bird, you will increase your chances of keeping birds in a specific area.

The Electronic Call Bird

Quality Wildlife Services (see appendix A) makes an electronic call bird called Total Recall. It is a small device that hangs on a tree with a photocell that activates a recording of a quail's call. This electronic call bird has three different settings:

Setting #1 calls for 7 minutes at dawn and then calls every 2 1/2 hours until dusk. Use this setting for quail that have been pre-released.

Setting #2 is used for field trials and shooting preserves, and it works well for training. It calls for 7 minutes every 30 minutes from dawn to dusk. Use this setting to keep birds together when you are working the same birds frequently.

Setting #3 emits a 7-minute call at dawn and dusk. Use this setting in combination with the Johnny House to help call birds back to the pen.

If you use the Total Recall, you may find the following tips helpful:

- Younger birds recall best; however, they should be old enough—about twelve weeks—to be through their juvenile molt.
- Quail do not recall well in the spring because pairs are mating.
- Release birds in such a way that they don't fly out of range of the caller.
- Spread feed around the area of the caller. Use the same feed that the birds are eating so that they recognize it as food.

Quail Feeders

Feeding quail encourages them to stay around. You can build a simple and inexpensive feeder, using the design of the feeders used at the Blue Mountain Wildlife Demonstration Area, Booneville, Arkansas, where the National Brittany Championships are currently held. Use it in combination with the Total Recall to improve success in keeping coveys on your training grounds. It also works well in the spring when quail do not recall.

The feeder consists of a freestanding circle of wire with a 2-foot length of PVC pipe suspended, vertically, through the middle. The PVC pipe holds the birdseed, and the wire circle keeps predators out.

Rabbit-shield garden fence—about 28 inches wide—works well for the wire part of the feeder. Cut a 6-foot length, join the two ends to form a circle, and secure them with wire or plastic ties.

You may use thin-walled, 4-inch-diameter PVC pipe cut in a 2-foot length. Glue a cap on one end. Turn the PVC pipe so that the pipe is vertical and the cap is at the bottom. Drill four evenly spaced holes into the sidewalls of the cap, using a 7/16-inch drill bit. Drill a second set of holes just above the cap, creating two alternating rows of four evenly spaced holes.

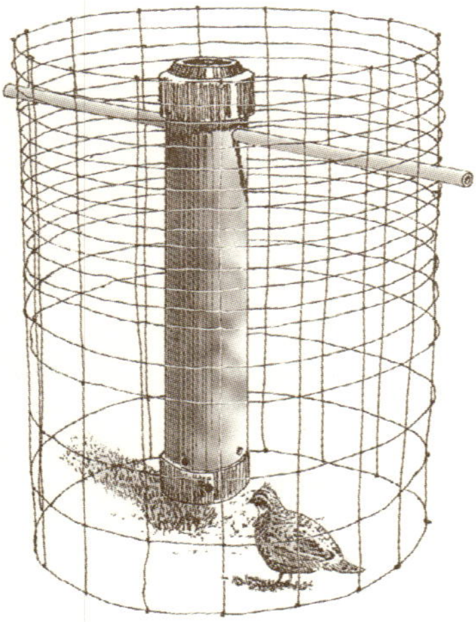

Quail Feeder

Place a second cap on the top of the PVC pipe for the lid, which you will remove when you fill the feeder.

To hang the feeder, you will need a 30-inch length of narrow pipe. Use 1/2-inch conduit because it is easy to cut with a pipe cutter. Drill holes through both sides of the PVC feeder just below the lid. The holes should be large enough for the conduit to slide through easily. Hang the feeder from the conduit and position it in the middle of the wire circle. The larger wire openings should be at the bottom. Hang the feeder about 2 to 3 inches off the ground. Use wire or plastic ties to secure the conduit to the wire circle. It is a good idea to spray-paint the PVC pipe with camouflage colors and patterns.

PRE-RELEASING SYSTEM FOR QUAIL

You can build a simple and inexpensive release system based on a design that the late Dick Keenan developed and has successfully used for thirty years at the Flying Feather Shooting Preserve in Guys Mills, Pennsylvania.

Construct a pen using four metal or wood fence posts and 2x4-inch turkey wire that is approximately 5 feet x 5 feet x 3 feet high. Dick used 3x5-foot chain-link gates that he clamped together to form a 5x3-foot-high pen. Find an out-of-the-way place that is near a tree line or hedgerow and clear the ground down to bare dirt before setting up the pen. Place a bottle waterer and feeding trough inside the pen about 1 foot from the fence. Fill the waterer with fresh water and put a mixture of cracked corn and quail feed—the same kind of feed the birds have been eating—in the trough feeder. Next, create a natural shelter for the birds by sliding sticks and branches horizontally through the openings in the fence, beginning at about 12 inches from the ground. Keep the lower 10 to 12 inches open so the birds can easily move around inside the pen.

Once the shelter looks natural, lay plastic across the top of the pile to keep the birds and feed dry and place more branches on top of the plastic to weight it down and hold it in place. The final construction step is to put wire over the top of the pen, which keeps the climbing predators—raccoons, skunks, and so forth—from getting to the birds. The purpose of the pen is to give the birds time to develop their independence. Unlike Johnny Houses and feeders that make the birds dependent, the pen provides temporary food and shelter while the birds learn survival skills. Once the birds learn how to survive, they leave the pen for habitat of their choosing.

Initially, the birds stay around the waterer and feeder and learn to hide under the branches in the pen. However, if they start exploring, or if they are scattered by a predator, the pen may not be enough to encourage them to return. Use an electronic call bird or a live bird to coax them back. For a live bird, build a small box out of hardware cloth with a metal or wooden top (to keep out the rain) and a door. Add water and feed to last at least a week, attach the box to a tree, and put a male quail in the box.

Once the pen is complete and the call bird is in place, load twenty to twenty-five quail into a chick crate (wooden box) that is about 8 inches high with a sliding door across the front.

The birds should be at least twelve weeks old so that they have their adult feathers and are mature enough to call. Position the crate against the fence, slide the door open, and leave quietly. The birds have to walk through the turkey wire or chain-link and across the feed to gain their freedom.

During the first week, do not disturb the birds. The feed and the call bird keep them near the pen. Early in the second week, remove the chick crate. If you are using a call bird, put a fresh bird in the call box and add water and feed as necessary. The released birds are learning to eat seeds and bugs and to hide from predators. They return to the pen less and less, but the call bird keeps them in the area. By the third week, the birds have left the pen for habitat of their choosing. Remove the waterer and feeder. Now, you are ready to start working your dogs on these birds, but be careful not to put too much pressure on them. If you work the birds too much, the feed and call bird will not be enough to keep them in the area.

Pre-releasing System for Quail

APPENDIX C

Scent – A Discussion of Game Birds and Bird Dogs

Below is an interview by Martha Greenlee with physical anthropologists Dr. Mike Siegel and Dr. Tim Smith. Mike and Tim conduct professional research on the anatomy and physiology of the head in a variety of animals, and, more importantly, they are avid bird hunters. Mike and Tim enjoy spending hours talking about their dogs' behaviors after a hunt. While they made it clear that they could not back up a discussion about scent with science (results of field or laboratory studies), they would bring their expertise in anatomy and physiology into the discussion. In preparation for this interview, Mike recommended that Martha read H. B. C. Pollard's classic book on scent, *The Mystery of Scent* (Eyre and Spottiswoode, London, 1937). This book was invaluable in preparing for the interview, and she has quoted sections from it in the discussion.

SCENT

Will scenting be good today? This is a question hunters often ask themselves before going afield. Once in the field, our dogs tell us when scenting is good by pointing their game confidently and at good distances. Our dogs tell us when scenting is bad by bumping birds or going birdless. While scent may seem unpredictable, we can learn to recognize good scenting conditions from poor ones by understanding the factors that affect scent. But before we can talk about conditions, we should understand how scent behaves and that it is a chemical substance.

Martha—Bird hunters often describe scent as behaving like smoke, rising and being carried by wind. I want to begin by reading a description of scent from Pollard's book because it is such a great analogy.

". . . consider a minute droplet of eucalyptus oil no bigger than a pin's head dropped on the surface of a bowl of warm water in a room with a dry warm atmosphere.

The oil spreads out into a typical film on which the familiar rainbow colors of an oil film can be discerned. It spreads itself as thin and flat and wide as it can and in a very short time represents a film of oil only one or two molecules thick. From the surface of the water, molecules of water vapor are continuously pouring upward into the dry air. Molecules of oil of eucalyptus cling to these water vapor molecules, and in a relatively short time the oil will be completely evaporated from the water surface and widely perceptible as scent in all parts of the room."

Mike—Perfect, and it was written over sixty years ago.

Martha—But what is scent exactly?

Mike—Scent is a chemical substance. It is something that can be volatile [airborne], and is usually carried on moisture in the air.

Martha—Bird hunters know that moisture—humidity—is important for good scenting conditions, but why is this true?

Tim—Odorants are simply molecules, suspended within some medium. They might be in water—we would say dissolved in water, or in the air. I suspect, but I don't know for sure, that humid air is simply less turbulent than dry air. Odorant molecules may simply travel faster in dry air because they are more likely to travel quickly in plumes [featherlike formations]. Humidity may make odor plumes less dispersed, but this is an intuitive guess.

Mike—One winter day a few years ago, Tim and I hunted when the wind chill was minus 20 degrees and the air temperature was 4 or 5 degrees. We saw four or five dogs have great difficulty finding birds that we knew were there. Later in the day we went through those spots and, sure enough, we found birds there. Our guess was that a combination of extreme cold and very low humidity caused a rapid dispersal of the scent. Whatever scent was there was immediately gone.

Martha—What other factors besides humidity influence scent? Air temperature, ground temperature, wind, sunlight, rain?

Mike—All of them. They are all variables that interact with each other. Humidity is telling us how much water is in the air. Air and ground temperature, wind, sunlight, and rain all influence how rapidly the scent disperses into the air. This means that hunting conditions are constantly changing. Think about a typical field trial. In the first few braces we aren't seeing any bird contact. Suddenly, it is a different place. Sunlight heats up the air. The wind picks up. All these variables you have listed are interdependent on each other.

Game Bird Scent

Bird hunters often use terms such as "body scent" and "foot scent" to describe different kinds of bird scents. Mike and Tim prefer the terms "air scent" and "ground scent" to distinguish scent that is in the air from scent that is on the ground. Generally, "air scent" comes from the bird's body, but it can also come from the bird's feet or droppings. Generally, "ground scent" comes from any part of the bird including feathers, feet, or droppings that comes in contact with the ground or vegetation.

Mike and Tim believe that factors influencing scent—humidity, temperature, wind, sunlight, rain—are important to consider when describing different kinds of scent, because they affect the volatility of scent and how widely and rapidly it is dispersed. For instance, in most conditions, foot scent is ground scent. Foot scent remains on the ground because it is protected from the wind by vegetation. But, in some conditions foot scent becomes airborne, so now it is air scent. How rapidly ground scent becomes air scent depends on volatility. Using terms based on parts of the bird to describe different kinds of scent can be faulty, since scent is constantly changing.

Martha—Pollard describes four different groups of scent that animals have.

"First, the true 'scent' or pad secretion—true trail scent which is hunted by other animals . . . ; secondly, the specific animal smell or body odor of the animal usually secreted by the anal or other specialized glands . . . ; thirdly, a special, seasonal sex scent secretion . . . ; lastly, a 'waste product' or urine scent which may carry all or any of the others at various stages of their manufacture."

If you were to guess, what would be the different types of scent that birds have?

Mike—We know many birds have preening glands that produce oil which they use for temperature regulation and other things like maintaining feathers. Other birds such as doves produce powder.

Tim—Secretions may have odors, so when a bird spreads the oil on its feathers, the feathers carry the scent. Every time a bird spreads its feathers, it releases scent through feather particles that come off the bird. If the bird doesn't want to be detected and tightly folds its feathers, it releases very little scent.

Martha—Is this why it is harder for dogs to find birds early in the morning before they are moving around?

Tim—Yes. A bird that isn't moving—one that has been in one spot for a long time—has a better chance of going undetected than a bird that is moving. There are two reasons. First, if the bird isn't moving, it doesn't release much into the air. Second, if the bird isn't moving, it doesn't leave a trail on the ground.

Mike—Think about a handkerchief. If I take a handkerchief out of my pocket and shake it, a lot of particles are dispersed. This is just one example of what can happen when a bird fluffs its feathers. As the bird moves around, it also leaves a trail on the ground from its feathers, feet, and droppings.

Martha—So birds give off scent from their feathers, feet, and droppings. What about their breath? I know a lot of hunters believe a dog smells the bird's breath because a dog can be retrieving a dead bird and stop and point a live bird.

Mike—I hate to fly in the face of an embedded myth, but a pheasant that weighs a couple of pounds has a lot of feathers on it, and these feathers give off a huge amount of scent whether the bird is alive or dead. Compare this to its tiny beak breathing in and out.

Tim—I agree. I think it has more to do with the static background. When the dog is walking with the bird in his mouth, the scent of the bird isn't changing. It just hangs there, and it is always the same. Anything else out there is a new stimulus, possibly a different type of scent, very possibly a stronger scent, which is in contrast to this static background.

Mike—How about this analogy: I'm walking and the light is dim. I've adjusted to what is out there, to this constant dimness. If a flashbulb goes off, I'll see it. It could be a good distance away, but I'll see it because it is in contrast to the background that is constant. If the dog has a bird in his mouth, the amount of scent isn't changing because the bird is dead.

Martha—Now, I'm going to change the subject because I want to ask about air washing. Can you explain what happens when a bird is air washed?

Mike—I've never liked this term. I don't know what air washing means. The scent is still there; it just isn't as strong.

Martha—Let me give you a specific example: I have two quail. I hold the first quail in my hand, shake it, and throw it down in the grass in front of me. I release the second bird into the air, and it flies and lands at the far end of the field. I would call the second bird *air washed.*

Mike—Okay. Think about two glasses of tea. I pour one glass of tea on the ground right here in front of me. Next, I hold the other glass and throw the tea through the air. Now, there is a concentration of scent on the ground around the first bird—where the tea was poured—but the spot on the ground where the second bird landed is not saturated with scent because the tea went through the air.

Tim—And, if you went out and found the second bird and threw it down on the ground, it would smell just as strong as the first bird. By throwing the bird down, you have created a concentration of scent in the air and on the ground.

Bird Dogs

Bird hunters often use the terms *trailing* and *tracking* to describe how dogs work scent, but Mike and Tim feel these terms are too close by definition to be useful. Instead, they believe that the emphasis should be on the volatility of the scent and the manner in which the dogs hunt. Since low volatility (slow dispersion) scents remain on the ground, dogs work these scents with low heads. High volatility (rapid dispersion) scents are airborne, and dogs work these scents with high heads. During a hunt, a dog may move from air scent to ground scent and back to air scent. We often see this during a relocation. The dog locates game by air scent, establishing point with a high head. After a flushing attempt, the dog is relocated, and he drops his head to work ground scent. Once he pins the bird and is taken on, he continues to hunt by constantly adjusting to different scent cues and changing scent conditions.

Martha—We've talked generally about scent and more specifically about game bird scent, but what are the mechanics of scent for the dog?

Tim—Scent is only scent to a dog if the dog has the built-in receptors. This is why humans miss out on a lot of scents dogs smell because we don't have these receptors.

When the dog inhales, these chemical substances are dissolved in the mucous surface of the nasal passages, thus coming in contact with the appropriate receptors.

Martha—What happens to the dog when the scenting conditions are constantly changing?

Tim—These variables can make a dog's job harder or easier.

Mike—Exactly. A dog will maximize olfaction. As scenting conditions change, a dog will adjust. Think about what happens as we start driving later in the afternoon as the sun is going down. If the sun is in our eyes, we change our driving style so that we can see better. And once the sun goes down, and it is twilight, we pay more attention to certain kinds of things to maximize our driving safety. In the same way, dogs are constantly trying to maximize their abilities to find birds.

Martha—Earlier, we talked about a dog that points a live bird with a dead bird in his mouth. This is an impressive feat.

Mike—Of course it is, but remember—a dead bird is a shot bird, and it gives off a combination of scents, including blood. Think about what can happen when a dog hunts dead. A bird is down, which the dog didn't mark, and he is going to find it. The hunter says, "Dead, hunt dead." Then, *wham*, the dog goes on point. This is a different bird than the one he has been hunting for. The dog knows that he is looking for a dead bird because he has been trained to hunt dead. But the live bird gets his attention, and he points it. He does not try to run in and grab it. He points it because he knows the difference between a live bird and one that has been shot.

Martha—Is there anything else that you think we would be interested in learning about our dogs?

Mike—One last thing to think about is that scent has temporal capabilities. When animals use sound to hunt their prey, they either hear it or they don't hear it. Once the sound is over, they have lost forever the ability to use that particular cue to locate their prey. When animals use scent to locate their prey, they can get a lot of information while they are smelling it—a lot more information than if they just heard a sound.

Martha—Wow, I never thought about it this way.

Mike—Take a nonproductive. Sometimes the dog is overpowered by scent from a feather pile on the ground. The dog goes on point. Now, it is a matter of training and experience for that dog to figure out that no bird is there. It is just a feather pile from a hawk kill. Temporal information is embedded in scent that is not in the other sense modalities. With scent, the dog smells the prey at the same time he is analyzing it, thinking about it, and perhaps deciding that it is old scent, i.e., no bird.

Martha—But isn't this like sight?

Tim—That is an interesting analogy because, presumably, what both scent and sight may have in common is spatial information. We get spatial cues—3-D relationships about where structures, animals, whatever, are in our surroundings. If I get really speculative and imagine what scent is for dogs, I see these hot spots all over the place. So, in addition to whatever they are getting from their visual sense, the environment is filled with these hot spots from different chemical stimuli, which they are receiving from their sense of smell.

Martha—What a great image. It is so easy for us to forget that our dogs are constantly being bombarded with all kinds of information from their noses as well as their eyes. Pollard addresses this topic in a wonderful paragraph about dogs' noses, and maybe this quote is a good way to conclude our discussion:

"Dogs are color-blind, seeing all colors as a monotone of different depths, but it is possible that scent to them is a perception of a range of differences as wide as those our optic nerves register. They see the world . . . in shades of light and shadow, but they know the world through their noses. We see the world in color, but have almost no noses. I am not sure that for real interest, apart from aesthetics, the dogs have not got the best of it."

Dr. Michael Siegel is a physical anthropologist and professor in the department of anthropology and orthodontics at the University of Pittsburgh. Dr. Timothy Smith is an associate professor in the School of Physical Therapy, Slippery Rock University, and adjunct research associate professor in the department of anthropology, University of Pittsburgh. They are currently conducting research on the Vomeronasal Organ (Jacobson's Organ).

(AN EARLIER VERSION OF THIS ARTICLE APPEARED IN *FIELD TRIAL MAGAZINE*, SUMMER ISSUE, 2004)

APPENDIX D

The Brittany in America

Learning About the AKC Brittany Standard

In 1934 the board of directors of the American Kennel Club formally recognized the Brittany spaniel breed and admitted it to the studbook. The AKC Brittany standard that was approved was a translation of the French standard, which with minor alterations had existed since it was first written in 1907. In 1946 the American Brittany Club appointed a committee to revise the standard. They instructed the committee to rewrite the standard so that a split between field and show Brittanys would not occur, as had happened with English and Irish setters. The new standard was written and approved by the American Kennel Club in 1966 and reaffirmed in 1977.

To further guard against a potential rift, the American Brittany Club promoted the dual dog (field and show) concept, and encouraged local Brittany clubs to hold both field and show events together. The objectives and purpose of the American Brittany Club are:

> To promote cooperation and friendship among the breeders and owners of Brittanys and to encourage higher standards in breeding, training, and showing of Brittanys in the field and in the show ring; to discourage the breed from becoming split into

groups of "field dogs" and "show dogs" and to strive to keep it forever a "dual dog."

You may ask, "What is the importance of the AKC Brittany standard, and why should a breed standard be applied to a Brittany that will never be in the show ring?" The introduction of this book contains a discussion of the manner in which strains—ultimately breeds—of scenting dogs developed. This development was based on a dog's ability to pursue game in the field. The next phase was to describe the physical characteristics of that particular strain. Breed standards were actually based on the working characteristics of particular strains of dogs. Physical characteristics such as size, color, eyes, ears, teeth, tail, and feet of working dogs were used to establish these standards.

First, backtrack for a moment and consider the development of dog breeds. During the latter part of the nineteenth century, change was rampant. The Industrial Revolution was impacting the order of rural life. Dog fanciers of that time realized that the breeds they admired, including all the various bird dogs, were disappearing. It is a fact that the various dog breeds were literally saved by dog shows. The various strains were studied, and the best dogs of each strain were selected. Then, standards for each breed were established. The era of purebred dogs had begun. As previously indicated, many of the breeds have split into field and show types, and this division includes most of the major sporting dog breeds. Now, go back to the question: Why should a breed standard be applied to the Brittany that will never be in the show ring?

Ben Williams (a well-known artist, photographer, writer, and upland bird guide) breeds his Brittanys for the terrain that he hunts—the wide-open ranges of his home state of Montana. He wants to keep the Brittany's temperament, but he wants dogs that are larger than the standard dictates. The dogs from his kennel will never be in the show ring.

Rigorous adherence to the AKC Brittany standard presents a dilemma. The history of the original French standard was based on the strain of Brittany that worked the cover, hunted the quarry, and retrieved the game. Times have changed, and so have the areas where people hunt and field-trial the Brittany. The dual dog concept is important for the breed, and the standard should be used as a guideline. However, tolerance should be the watchword for dogs that will never enter the show ring. The future of the breed depends on those who own and breed Brittanys and on their love of the dog, both in the field and in the show ring.

The AKC Brittany Standard

OFFICIAL STANDARD FOR THE BRITTANY

GENERAL APPEARANCE—
A compact, closely knit dog of medium size; a leggy dog having the appearance, as well as the agility, of a great ground coverer. Strong, vigorous, energetic, and quick of movement. Ruggedness, without clumsiness, is a characteristic of the breed. He can be tailless or have a tail docked to approximately four inches.

SIZE, PROPORTION, SUBSTANCE—

Height: 17 1/2 to 20 1/2 inches, measured from the ground to the highest point of the shoulders. Any Brittany measuring under 17 1/2 inches or over 20 1/2 inches shall be disqualified from dog show competition.

Weight: Should weigh between 30 and 40 pounds. Proportion: So leggy is he that his height at the shoulders is the same as the length of his body.

Body Length: Approximately the same as the height when measured at the shoulders. Body length is measured from the point of the forechest to the rear of the rump. A long body should be heavily penalized.

Substance: Not too light in bone, yet never heavy-boned and cumbersome.

HEAD-EXPRESSION–
Alert and eager, but with the soft expression of a bird dog.

Eyes: Well set in head. Well protected from briars by a heavy, expressive eyebrow. A prominent, full, or popeye should be heavily penalized. It is a serious fault in a dog that must face briars. Skull should be well chiseled under the eyes, so that the lower lid is not pulled back to form a pocket or haw that would catch seeds, dirt, and weed dust. Preference should be for the darker-colored eyes, though lighter shades of amber should not be penalized. Light and mean-looking eyes should be heavily penalized.

Ears: Set high, above the level of the eyes. Short and triangular, rather than pendulous, reaching about half the length of the muzzle. Should lie flat and close to the head, with the tip rounded very slightly. Ears well covered with dense, but relatively short hair, and with little fringe.

Skull: Medium length, rounded, very slightly wedge-shaped, but evenly made. Width, not quite as wide as the length and never so broad as to appear coarse, or so narrow as to appear racy. Well defined, but gently sloping stop. Median line rather indistinct. The occiput only apparent to the touch. Lateral walls well rounded. The Brittany should never be "apple-headed," and he should never have an indented stop.

Muzzle: Medium length, about two-thirds the length of the skull, measuring the muzzle from the tip to the stop, and the skull from the occiput to the stop. Muzzle should taper gradually in both horizontal and vertical dimensions as it approaches the nostrils. Neither a Roman nose nor a dish-face is desirable. Never broad, heavy or snipy.

Nose: Nostrils well open to permit deep breathing of air and adequate scenting. Tight nostrils should be penalized. Never shiny. Color should be fawn, tan, shades of brown or deep pink. A black nose is a disqualification. A two-tone or butterfly nose should be penalized.

Lips: Tight, the upper lip overlapping the lower jaw just to cover the lower lip. Lips dry, so that feathers will not stick. Drooling to be heavily penalized. Flews to be penalized.

Bite: A true scissors bite. Overshot or undershot jaw to be heavily penalized.

NECK, TOPLINE, BODY–

Topline: Medium length. Free from throatiness, though not a serious fault unless accompanied by dewlaps, strong without giving the impression of being over muscled. Well set into sloping shoulders. Never concave or ewe-necked.

Topline: Slight slope from the highest point of the shoulders to the root of the tail.

Chest: Deep, reaching the level of the elbow. Neither so wide nor so rounded as to disturb the placement of the shoulders and elbows. Ribs well sprung. Adequate heart room provided by depth as well as width. Narrow or slab-sided chests are a fault.

Back: Short and straight. Never hollow-, saddle-, sway-, or roach-backed. Slight drop from the hips to the root of the tail.

Flanks: Rounded. Fairly full. Not extremely tucked up, or flabby and falling. Loins short and strong. Distance from last rib to upper thigh short, about three to four finger widths. Narrow and weak loins are a fault. In motion, the loin should not sway sideways, giving a zigzag motion to the back, wasting energy.

Tail: Tailless to approximately four inches, natural or docked. The tail not to be so long as to affect the overall balance of the dog. Set on high, actually an extension of the spine at about the same level. Any tail substantially more than four inches shall be severely penalized.

FOREQUARTERS; SHOULDERS–

Shoulder blades should not protrude too much, not too wide apart, with perhaps two thumbs' width between. Sloping and muscular. Blade and upper arm should form nearly a ninety-degree angle. Straight shoulders are a fault. At the shoulders the Brittany is slightly higher than at the rump.

Front Legs: Viewed from the front, perpendicular, but not set too wide. Elbows and feet turning neither in nor out. Pasterns slightly sloped. Down in pasterns is a serious fault.

Leg bones clean, graceful, but not too fine. Extremely heavy bone is as much a fault as spindly legs. One must look for substance and suppleness. Height at elbows should approximately equal distance from elbow to withers.

Feet: Should be strong, proportionately smaller than the spaniels', with close-fitting, well-arched toes and thick pads. The Brittany is not "up on his toes." Toes not heavily feathered. Flat feet, splayed feet, paper feet, etc., are to be heavily penalized. An ideal foot is halfway between the hare and the cat foot. Dewclaws may be removed.

HINDQUARTERS–

Broad, strong, and muscular, with powerful thighs and well-bent stifles, giving the angulation necessary for powerful drive.

Hind Legs: Stifles well bent. The stifle should not be so angulated as to place the hock joint far out behind the dog. A Brittany should not be condemned for straight stifle until the judge has checked the dog in motion from the side. The stifle joint should not turn out, making a cow hock. Thighs well feathered but not profusely, halfway to the hock. Hocks—that is, the back pasterns—should be moderately short, pointing neither in nor out, perpendicular when viewed from the side. They should be firm when shaken by the judge.

Feet: Same as front feet.

COAT–

Dense, flat, or wavy, never curly. Texture neither wiry nor silky. Ears should carry little fringe. The front and hind legs should have some feathering, but too little is definitely preferable to too much. Dogs with long or profuse feathering or furnishings shall be so severely penalized as to effectively eliminate them from competition.

Skin: Fine and fairly loose. A loose skin rolls with briars and sticks, thus diminishing punctures or tearing. A skin so loose as to form pouches is undesirable.

COLOR–

Orange and white or liver and white in either clear or roan patterns. Some ticking is desirable. The orange or liver is found in the standard parti-color or piebald patterns. Washed out colors are not desirable. Tricolors are allowed but not preferred. A tricolor is a liver-and-white dog with classic orange markings on eyebrows, muzzle, and cheeks, inside the ears, and under the tail; freckles on the lower legs are orange. Anything exceeding the limits of these markings shall be severely penalized. Black is a disqualification.

GAIT–
When at a trot, the Brittany's hind foot should step into or beyond the print left by the front foot. Clean movement, coming and going, is very important, but most important is side gait, which is smooth, efficient, and ground-covering.

TEMPERAMENT–
A happy, alert dog, neither mean nor shy.

Registering Your Brittany

When you pick up your new pup from the breeder, you should get an AKC registration form from the breeder. You may ask, "Why should my pup be registered?" A simple reason could be pride of ownership in having a registered dog. More important, if you want to compete in AKC licensed field trials or dog show events, your dog *must* be registered. If you want to breed or sell your dog, your dog should be registered so that a prospective buyer knows that your dog is purebred. The AKC paper is proof of your dog's bloodlines. Another important registration agency is the American Field, which operates the Field Dog Stud Book (FDSB). During the course of a year, the American Field holds licensed field trials that have been sanctioned only by that organization. If your dog wins a championship, he must be registered in the FDSB in order to receive the title of champion.

Reading a Pedigree

When you get your new pup, you may be given a chart that lists the sire, the dam, the grandparents, the great-grandparents, and so forth. This piece of paper is known as a *pedigree* and is usually prepared by the breeder. The authenticity of the names, dates, and titles (field and show champions) of your pup's ancestry is based on the knowledge of the person who signed the pedigree. For a fee, you can get a "signed and stamped with a seal" copy of your pup's pedigree from the American Kennel Club.

In addition to tracing your pup's ancestry, his pedigree also includes the number of field and show champions in his background. When you pick a pup, you should consider his parents and grandparents. If you do not already know his background, the pedigree will give you an indication of whether he is from field or show lines.

Different registries use different title designations, so pay attention to the registry. "CH" on an AKC pedigree means that the dog is a show champion. "CH" on an FDSB pedigree means that the dog has won an American Field championship.

Following is a list of titles that may be earned under the AKC registry:

DC	Dual Champion (field and show)
CH	Champion (show)
FC	Field Champion
AFC	Amateur Field Champion
NAGDC	National Amateur Gun Dog Champion
NGDC	National Open Gun Dog Champion
NAFC	National Amateur Field Champion
NFC	National Field Champion

Bibliography

Amateur Field Trial Clubs of America, Inc. *Guidelines to Field Trial Procedure and Judicial Practice.* Amateur Field Trial Clubs of America, Inc., 1988.

American Kennel Club. *The Complete Dog Book,* 18th Edition. New York: Howell Book House, 1992.

American Kennel Club. *Registration and Field Trial Rules and Standard Procedures for Pointing Dogs.* The American Kennel Club, 1993.

Bailey, Joan. *How to Help Gun Dogs Train Themselves.* Portland, Oregon: Swan Valley Press, 1993.

Bissell, Nicky, ed. *The Official Book of the Brittany Spaniel.* American Brittany Club, 1972.

Bissell, Nicky. *Pointing Dog Training: Especially the Continental Breeds.* Sherwood, Oregon: B. B. Supplies, Inc.

Crangle, Earl C. *Pointing Dogs: Their Training and Handling.* Milan, New Hampshire: Androscoggin Publishing, Inc., 2000.

Hammond, Ralph B. and Robert D. Hammond. *Training and Hunting the Brittany Spaniel.* New York: A. B. Barnes & Company, 1971.

Long, Paul. *Training Pointing Dogs: All the Answers to Your Questions.* New York: Lyons & Burford, 1974.

Ortega y Gasset, Jose. *Meditations on Hunting.* New York: Charles Scribner's Sons, 1972.

Riddle, Maxwell. *The New Complete Brittany,* 2nd Edition. New York: Macmillan Publishing Company, 1987.

Rutherford, Clarice and David H. Neil. *How to Raise a Puppy You Can Live With,* 3rd Edition. New York: MJF Books, 1999.

Robinson, Jerome B. *The Ultimate Guide to Bird Dog Training.* New York: The Lyons Press, 2000.

Tarrant, Bill. *Best Way to Train Your Gun Dog: The Delmar Smith Method.* New York: David McKay Company, Inc., 1977.

Tarrant, Bill. *How to Hunt Birds with Gun Dogs.* Mechanicsburg, Pennsylvania: Stackpole Books, 1994.

Wolters, Richard A. *Game Dog: A Concise New Training Method,* 2nd Edition. New York: Dutton Books, the Penguin Group, 1995.

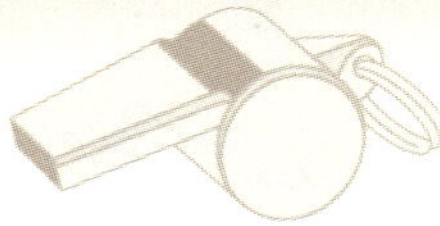

Glossary of Terms

Aggression: The unprovoked attack by a dog that willfully attempts to go after another dog with the intent to do physical harm.

Backing: A dog stopping and standing at the sight of another dog that is on rigid point.

Beeper collar: A collar that emits a beeping noise. Different modes include single and double tone, run and point, point only, and so forth.

Bird bag: A nylon bag with a mesh front for ventilation designed for carrying birds.

Bird launcher: A spring-loaded metal box with air holes that launches a bird into the air.

Blinking: The avoidance of game; when a dog finds birds and leaves or points birds and leaves.

Breaking process: The teaching of a dog to be steady-to-wing-and-shot.

Broke: Steady-to-wing-and-shot.

Bumping: Deliberately crowding a bird and causing it to fly.

Check-cord: A stiff rope, about 1/2 inch in diameter, about 12 feet long, with a swivel snap at one end.

Dual dog: A dog that is an AKC show and field champion.

E-collar: An electronic training collar.

Edge: A tree line, ravine, and so forth that creates a line for the dog to hunt.

Establishing point: A dog that is assuming the pointing position.

Field trial: Competitive event for dogs.

Flagging: Tail movement when the dog is on point.

Force-retrieve: Using force to teach a dog to retrieve.

Green-broke: Recently broke.

Gun-shy: Being afraid of gunfire.

"Here": A command to "come to me" or "go with me."
Honoring: *See* backing.
Identification collar: A collar with the owner's name (not the dog's name), city, state, telephone number, and the phrase "call collect."
Objective: Likely cover for holding birds (a clump of brush, hedgerow, or distant tree line) that a dog runs to and hunts.
Pattern: A specific way of hunting the terrain.
Pointing: A dog rigidly standing to indicate the presence and position of game.
Puttering: Dawdling.
Roading: Conditioning a dog by letting him pull in a harness. The harness is attached to a moving vehicle (ATV, bicycle, sled, and so forth) or a horse.
Show dog: A dog that competes in the show ring.
Silhouette: A wood or metal cutout of a dog on point, used as a substitute for a real dog when teaching a dog to back.
Stacking: Posing a dog to show his conformation and style.
Stake: An individual field trial event.
Stakeout chain: A chain-and-stake combination used to tie out one or more dogs.
Steady-to-wing: A dog remaining on point during the flight of a bird.
Steady-to-wing-and-shot: A dog remaining on point during the flight of a bird and remaining on point after the bird is shot.
Stealing point: A dog that moves in front of another dog that has already established point.
Stop-to-flush: A dog stopping at the flush of birds he did not see or smell.
Taking out a bird: A dog that bumps or flushes a bird that he should have pointed.
Trailing: One dog following another dog.
Training collar: A leather collar that is attached to the check-cord; used in yard work.
"Whoa": A command used to tell a dog to "stop and stand still."
Yard work: Formal training that takes place when the dog is under control in a controlled environment.

Index